D0054248

Praise for *365 Prescriptions for the Soul* by Dr. Bernie S. Siegel

"Bernie Siegel dispenses spiritual medicine that's good for you, and feels good too! I highly recommend these daily doses of eternal wisdom."

— Marianne Williamson, author of *Everyday Grace*

"Bernie is one of the world's most respected doctors. I would pay close attention to any prescription he offers. I read from this each day."

— Wayne Dyer, author of *Getting in the Gap*

"Dr. Siegel's soul medicine is dispensed in perfect doses to uplift, inspire, enlighten, and heal you. As always, Bernie's wisdom and love gave me goose bumps, or should I say god-bumps. Buy a carton of this medicine-in-a-book and administer it to everyone you love."

— Joan Borysenko, PhD, author of
Inner Peace for Busy People

Praise for *101 Exercises for the Soul* by Dr. Bernie S. Siegel

"Another loving, wise, practical, and life-changing book from Dr. Bernie. This step-by-step fitness guide is for the part of you that has wings."

— Rachel Naomi Remen, MD, author of
Kitchen Table Wisdom

"From one of America's master healers, a practical guide that provides a step-by-step entry into a healthier, more fulfilling way of being. Siegel is a genius for inspiring people to reach beyond themselves and attain what they thought not possible."

— Larry Dossey, MD, author of *Healing Words*

"This simple book has all the wisdom you need to live life from your best self. Bernie has the gift of taking complex ideas and making them simple and accessible. Follow his workout plan, and you'll create a life more wonderful than any you might ever have imagined."

— Joan Borysenko, PhD, author of *Inner Peace for Busy People*

"I have always admired Dr. Bernie Siegel as one of the most remarkable minds of our time. He combines an analytical scientific mind with a deep knowingness of spirituality. His *101 Exercises for the Soul* will help you understand and learn from that part of you which is the ultimate and supreme genius and mirrors the wisdom of the universe."

— Deepak Chopra, author of *The Book of Secrets*

"A beautiful, heartfelt book by a legendary physician to help you nurture mind, body, and soul."

— Judith Orloff, MD, author of *Second Sight* and *Positive Energy*

"I knew Bernie Siegel's latest book, *101 Exercises for the Soul*, was magical when I opened it at random and 'happened' to turn to the chapter titled 'Furry Friends.' Our beautiful sixteen-year-old cat had died just the day before, and here was an entire chapter of Bernie's warm, accessible writing ready to provide solace and spiritual connection with Max, whom we loved so much."

— Sue Patton Thoele, author of
Growing Hope and *The Courage to Be Yourself*

"Bernie Siegel is a rare jewel of a teacher and healer. He is wise, loving, humorous, clear, mature, grounded, and ultimately practical. He knows how to reach people where they are touched. *101 Exercises for the Soul* will bring you insight, inspiration, release, and practical tools to be well, happy, and creative. Go, Bernie!"

— Alan Cohen, author of *I Had It All the Time*

A BOOK
of
miracles

A BOOK

of

miracles

Inspiring True Stories of Healing, Gratitude, and Love

Dr. Bernie S. Siegel

with Andrea Hurst

FOREWORD BY DEEPAK CHOPRA

New World Library
Novato, California

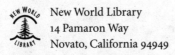
New World Library
14 Pamaron Way
Novato, California 94949

Text design by Tona Pearce Myers

Library of Congress Cataloging-in-Publication Data available upon
request.

First printing, September 2011
ISBN 978-1-57731-968-9
Printed in Canada on 100% postconsumer-waste recycled paper

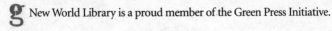 New World Library is a proud member of the Green Press Initiative.

10 9 8 7 6 5 4 3 2 1

Contents

Foreword

*B*ernie Siegel began his writing career twenty-five years ago, and from the outset he didn't shy away from miracles. The title of his first book — *Love, Medicine & Miracles* (1986) — flaunted his disagreement with mainstream medicine. An MD who advised more love as a path to healing would have been in enough trouble. Opening the possibility of miracles was grounds for dismissal. In this new book, Bernie reaffirms his original beliefs, and with a lifetime's wisdom and experience, he trusts in miracles more than ever.

His certainty implies that he has followed a path and the path bore fruit. These pages offer evidence that miracles are based on an "intelligent, loving, conscious" source. These qualities were not invented by the human mind: they are universal; they are innate in the construction of creation. The minute you make such an assertion, you court science's disapproval, but Bernie was trained in scientific medicine, and he understands that disapproval is usually a screen. Behind the mask, science cannot tell us how consciousness arose, why life evolved from inert atoms and molecules, or even how we perceive a vibrant world when the interior of the brain is utterly without light, sound, touch, taste, or smell. How can it be that an atom of oxygen, floating randomly in the atmosphere, gets inhaled and, the instant it crosses the blood-brain barrier, becomes part of an intelligent system? It cannot be that oxygen atoms are already thinking, feeling, and doing all the other things that the brain does. So what is the process that differentiates a lump of sugar in a sugar bowl, an object not well known for thinking, and the sugar (glucose) that is the brain's sole food? Science cannot give a viable answer, and so, despite dismissal and disapproval, one must look elsewhere.

Bernie has looked to an expanded science, as we might call it, where spirituality meets the real world, the world of human suffering and human triumph. The hundred billion neurons in the human brain embody that mysterious meeting point. Miracles occur where the invisible possibilities of life unfold as realities. We already know that the brain is where meaning and purpose are born. For centuries, it was assumed that *higher* meaning and *higher* purpose are born somewhere else — in the mind of God, perhaps, or through the extraordinary powers given to saints and prophets. Bernie understood from the start that this division between the natural and the supernatural was artificial. As a time-honored spiritual adage puts it, "Nothing is a miracle unless everything is a miracle." A speck of human DNA left out at noon on a hot summer day will wither and blow away in an hour, yet DNA has survived for billions of years, sustaining the most complex structure in creation without visible means of support. How did it evolve and thrive? Because life finds a way, guided by the universe's conscious, intelligent, creative impulse.

Miracles occur when you align yourself with that impulse. In the words of this book, "To me miracles are about our potential and what has been built into us." Yet there is only so much that the body can do on its own. Physical development unfolds automatically; it's a gift from the evolutionary past. Every time you resist catching a cold or fend off an allergen, your immune system relies upon its memory of the past. As a small gland in the middle of the chest, the thymus stores information about every disease that human beings have confronted over millions of years. So the antibodies produced by a two-year-old are an expression of humanity as a whole. The same is true of the thoughts you have today, the words you speak, the actions you take. They are yours and yet not yours. Through you, human life is looking for its next step in the long journey of self-discovery.

This book is a call to take an evolutionary leap not through some kind of automatic unfoldment but by using conscious choice. Love, intelligence, and creativity are seeds waiting to be touched and awakened. The more you touch them, the more they flourish. Bernie looks upon this evolutionary leap as a miracle, but it is also a survival mechanism in his eyes. Who can disagree? Looking out on a world ravaged by the absence of love, on machines of destruction employed in war, on medicine that takes care of people's bodies but cares little about people themselves, one yearns for a new insight that will create a shift away from a lack of love to an abundance of love. We don't have the luxury of calling this "soft" thinking; the fate of the human race depends on making connections where long-held divisions exist.

Because of his warmhearted style and his outreach to every kind of person who needs healing, one might overlook the deep roots of Bernie's worldview. First, there is the principle of nonduality, which holds that matter and energy, mind and matter, only appear to be different. Hiding behind the mask of materialism is one reality that embraces everything. Nonduality goes back five thousand years, to the origins of spirituality in ancient India. Second, there is the principle that we live in a conscious universe. This takes expression in, among many other places, Genesis, where God doesn't stand apart from his creation but fully enters into it. Third, there is the principle of evolution, which says that despite the appearance of a random universe governed by chance, creation gets increasingly more complex and life more advanced. Although Darwin is given the credit for proposing physical evolution (he didn't believe in any spiritual domain), the world's rich tradition of enlightenment expresses the principle of evolution through the soul.

Taking these three principles together, Bernie arrives at the conclusion reached by sages and seers in every age: consciousness comes first. It creates, governs, and controls all events in the material world, most especially in the human body. This is a sweeping conclusion, one that Bernie has held on to fervently and that he presents for others to witness in the stories that fill his new book. There will always be skeptics who resist this line of thought; in their worldview, materialism is the beginning and end of the story. But being open-minded about miracles has become more common, a surprising, often silent revolt against the theory that life is random and without purpose. In the worldview that this book expresses, anything is possible, and what makes the difference between a dream and reality is ourselves. Human beings live in a reality that seems complete but is only a fraction of what lies at our source. Unknown outcomes are simply those we haven't permitted ourselves to envision yet. Our awareness stands at the gate, permitting one outcome to emerge into the real world while denying entry to other ones.

Why do we restrict our reality in this way? Fear, disbelief, the heavy hand of materialism, ignorance of the wider possibilities — and then more fear. Ultimately, William Blake was right to say that we are shackled by "mind-forged manacles." It's slow going when an entrenched worldview decides to shift, and it happens only one person at a time. Bernie Siegel, having liberated his own awareness, devotes himself to freeing other people from their limitations. His efforts are gracious, intelligent, giving, and farsighted, as every reader of this book will soon discover.

— Deepak Chopra,
author of *The Seven Spiritual Laws of Success*

Introduction

Why, who makes much of miracles?
As to me I know of nothing else but miracles,
To me every hour of the light and dark is a miracle,
Every cubic inch of space is a miracle,
Every square yard of the surface of the earth is spread with
*   the same,*
Every foot of the interior swarms with the same.

— Walt Whitman

*M*any years ago, I would have defined miracles as something for which there was no explanation. That was my concept of miracles. So when patients would recover unexpectedly from disease, I would rationalize what mechanisms were present within the body that could explain their recovery.

Today, I realize that everything is a miracle. When you ask quantum physicists and astronomers to explain creation, they do not have all the answers. Life is a miracle, and it is derived from the intelligent, loving, conscious energy that created it. You can call it God or anything you want to, but the nature of life shows us it is intelligent and loving, or we wouldn't be able to survive a cut finger or an infection. Most of us do not stop to think about life on earth being a miracle.

To me, miracles are about our potential and what has been built into us to help us to survive. A botanist I read about called miracles "spontaneous reversals" because he saw how plants altered their genes to survive climate changes and diseases. Just think about the fact that a plant doesn't bleed to death every fall when the leaves drop off...it heals and survives.

Doctors call unexpected recoveries and cures "spontaneous remissions," but that wording makes you think it is luck and that the person had nothing to do with it. That is not true. All living things have the potential to create miracles. Studies and scans show that cancers come and go sometimes with no treatment. We need to study the personalities and learn the stories of the people whom we consider to have had a miraculous or self-induced healing.

I know people who have left their troubles to God, or who refused treatment to go home and make the world beautiful before they died. They did what made them happy — from getting a dog to building a wildlife habitat — and their letters to me later end with, "I didn't die, and now I'm so busy I'm killing myself. Help! Where do I go from here?" I do not limit miracles to only physical events like recovery from disease, because they occur in every aspect of life. Since consciousness is not limited to the body, or by time and space, it can have effects at a distance, too, and I will discuss some of these things when I present specific examples.

Someday I hope we will spend as much money exploring inner space and the wonders of the human body as we are currently spending exploring outer space. The secret lies within us, and yet we are afraid to go within because of our nature. It is time to stop fearing what lies within us and to achieve our true potential.

A true miracle is often defined as an event that defies the laws of nature. My mother referred to miracles as "God's redirections" from which something good would come. A television show you never knew existed alerts you to a medical condition you wouldn't have checked out otherwise; a kind stranger helps you change your tire before a flood; while you are sleeping a dog barks when he smells a fire. There is so much more to these occurrences than chance.

These events are more than coincidences. These are *miracles*.

In fact, even so-called "bad breaks" can be classified as miracles because so often they lead us in better directions. Years ago, arthritis threatened to end my career as a surgeon before it had even begun. The military turned me down for active duty, so I returned to Connecticut to attempt to practice surgery with a former associate. Almost immediately, the symptoms of my arthritis subsided, and I went on to practice medicine and become who I am today.

Rather than wishing for miracles to change the physical nature of life, my desire is for those miracles that change our experience of it. When we decide to make a difference in the world and create peace, love, and happiness for all living things... *that* will indeed be a miracle.

We are all living a miraculous story. When we are enlightened by it, we elevate ourselves and demonstrate loving, intelligent, conscious energy. To do so we must act, seek wisdom, and have devotion. Those are the qualities demonstrated by those who exceed expectations.

I read a wonderful article by Stacey Chiew, who wrote, "I believe each one of us holds the key that unlocks the door for miracles. Before you can do that, you need to know the password: Love. Miracles are the response to love expressed in us and to others. It is the extra ordinary healing power of our body, the amazing protective energy force that helps keep us safe, and the joy when prayers are answered."

I agree with Stacey that life is a miracle. We cannot, and probably never will, be able to explain creation and how intelligent, loving, conscious energy could create matter.

In this book I share some of my favorite stories, the gems garnered from my medical practice, the thousands of emails I receive, and my personal life experiences. During my many years working with patients, I feel I have become an expert on the prevalence and reality of miracles. My hope is that sharing these heartfelt experiences with you will ignite the spirit of hope and gratitude in your life. We all need to be aware of our potential and not see our attempt to achieve a miracle as a possible source of failure. Not everyone wins the lottery or goes to Lourdes and has miraculous healing, but some do. So why not learn from those who do and give it a try. I know you will enjoy and benefit from the attempt so don't fear taking responsibility and participating in the attempt.

A Book of Miracles is divided into fifteen sections, each consisting of stories of miracles, pertinent quotes, anecdotes, and my reflections. Every aspect of miracles is explored, from miracles of daily life to amazing stories of healing. I encourage you to look for and help create miracles every day. My hope is that this book will uplift, strengthen, and guide you on the miraculous journey called life.

CHAPTER ONE

Birth and Renewal

Birth is the sudden opening of a window, through which you look out upon a stupendous prospect. For what has happened? A miracle. You have exchanged nothing for the possibility of everything.

— William MacNeile Dixon

*T*he nature of life is a miracle. It is the intelligent, loving, conscious energy that is behind creation and understands that true creation begins when we have variety and not one type of living thing. Creation begins when we add another one.

Every child is a miracle. The sperm and egg meet, and from one cell a human being is created. The intelligence is present in every cell. It knows what it is and where it belongs. If a cell is misplaced in the embryo by changing its location, it will migrate back to the place and organ it belongs in and to. Every seed is filled with wisdom and knowledge. The seed of a plant can detect gravity so it knows which way to grow to find the sunlight, and it can even break through the pavement to make that happen.

Our minds also play a part in the miracle. Infertile women increase their chances of conceiving a baby when they join support groups and deal with their emotional issues and when they begin to visualize what they desire happening rather than being depressed and stressed over their desire to conceive. Fear and the stress response exist for our protection from threats to our life, but they suppress the body's ability to grow and heal when we continue to fear what we imagine or fantasize.

One of my support group members called me when she was in premature labor and feared aborting her fetus. When I went to the hospital to visit her, I could feel the room filled with fear and panic. I asked everyone to leave, and then I played calming music and guided her through imagery to relax her uterus and stop the contractions. Everything returned to normal in a short time, and she went on to deliver at full term and named her son after me. They were Irish, so his name is Brady, not Bernie. But that was close enough for me.

Babies Are Miraculous

BY TANYA F. CHERNOV

When my best friend, Rachel, called me one summer afternoon five years ago, I was terrified that she would be calling me from the hospital. Rachel had been suffering from debilitating bouts of ulcerative colitis for several years and had, in recent months, been barely able to function. Instead, when I answered the phone, she told me that she was unexpectedly pregnant. Knowing she needed all the support she could get, I screamed my elation into the phone, professing my love and excitement.

When we hung up, I let my fears come to the surface. Rachel had been so sick for so long, and I wondered how her poor body could possibly carry a baby. Rachel had been losing weight, losing blood volume, and suffering many terrible side effects from the medications that were keeping her alive. I was scared for her, and I was also scared for the baby because of all the harsh medications Rachel had been taking. Would she be able to carry to term? Would the baby be healthy? There was nothing I could do except be loving and supportive, no matter how strong my doubts and fears became.

The months passed, and instead of growing weaker, Rachel became healthy again. Each time I saw her, she looked more beautiful and healthy. She was strong and energetic, with color in her cheeks for the first time in years. As the first trimester passed into the second, Rachel felt incredible — she was free from all her colitis symptoms, as if the awful disease had never been a part of her life. She no longer needed any medications beyond prenatal vitamins. As if the baby growing inside her were made of healing qualities, Rachel's body responded accordingly, somehow returning to a miraculous level of health. Watching her belly grow and witnessing her body's recovery, I learned to trust that life will find a way — that the body is capable of sudden and miraculous changes when necessary. We joked that if this was how her colitis responded to pregnancy, then she'd want to be pregnant all the time, and her partner would be a very busy man!

In March, Rachel gave birth to a perfectly healthy, perfectly beautiful baby girl, named Linnea Spring. The joy of Linnea's birth was cut short only two weeks later when Rachel's colitis returned, exponentially more destructive than ever. With a newborn baby to take care of, Rachel's body quickly declined, her emotional state tumbling along with her physical condition. Rachel was admitted to the hospital with less than half the blood volume considered safe for a postpartum woman and having gained almost thirty pounds of edema. When I arrived at the hospital, I barely recognized Rachel. It seemed as if the moment her body knew that it had succeeded in creating new life, it began to recede into the darkness. I stayed with Rachel for the next two weeks as she was subjected to ineffective medications, treatments, and procedures.

Because hospitals are not always such friendly places for newborn babies, and because Linnea, still only weeks old, was being shuttled between family members wanting to help, Rachel did not get to see her brand-new daughter very often. She was getting worse, and we feared that this would be the end for her.

Finally, when it seemed that the only thing that could save Rachel's life would be a radical operation to remove her entire colon, we had an idea. Rachel was moved to the maternity ward, where she was reunited with her baby. The instant Rachel held her baby in her arms again, I saw that flash of color return to her cheeks. The three of us — Rachel, Linnea, and I — stayed in that hospital room for several days, each morning bringing a tinge of hope to Rachel's situation. With an experimental medication seemingly bringing her colitis into remission, my best friend's life returned to her.

Though her doctors will say the medication brought Rachel back from the brink of death, I know otherwise. Linnea saved Rachel's body during pregnancy, and she did it again when Rachel was so close to dying in the hospital. Rachel needed her baby to heal — not just once, but twice. Babies are miraculous even in the best of situations, but the power of the bond between mother and child is strong enough to defy death. I have been blessed to bear witness to this miracle for the last five years, as Linnea has grown into a precocious little girl, with a strong, healthy, and vibrant mother.

Anchored in the Arms of God

BY CHRISTIE GORSLINE

Nanook, our sailboat, ghosted into the bay wrapped in a thick blanket of humidity. Rick dropped the anchor and I furled the sails. The stillness was broken only by baritone reverberations that sounded like whales singing. We were sitting in the cockpit when rain peppered the sea, each drop piercing the surface like the needle of a sewing machine at full speed.

I raised my arms to the heavens in a gesture of celebration, gyrating in a rendition of a tribal dance. We offered our thanks for the sudden downpour. We'd been sailing the west coast of Mexico for three years, and nature's surprises still filled us with awe.

The torrent stopped within an hour. Reclining on the bow with a damp sail bag for a pillow, I watched the clouds play charades. A breeze rearranged them. A pirate? A banana. Light globes. Italy. So many shapes. A furious splashing off our stern interrupted my dream weaving.

A whale, her glistening back shining like a boulder in the bright sunshine, thrashed with an intensity that was alarming. Handing the binoculars to Rick, I said, "What do you think is wrong?"

He watched for a few minutes and said, "It looks like she's trying to shake something from her tail."

I sat in the corner of the cockpit, arms wrapped around my knees, squinting over the railing. Rick stood next to me. We watched in despair at the picture unfolding in front of us. It looked as though trash must be the culprit, and we felt somehow responsible.

As the minutes crept by, our attention turned to the whale's timing. She took breaks from her spasms at regular intervals. Two minutes of furious splashing were followed by thirty seconds of quiet. And it repeated. Again. And again. Even with the aid of high-powered binoculars, we couldn't identify the reason.

It went on for nearly an hour before the commotion stopped. It was Rick who figured out what we might be witnessing. "Holy mother of…," Rick said, handing me the binoculars.

"What is it?" I said, raising the binoculars to my eyes.

"*Es un milagro,*" Rick answered, his eyes glistening with unshed tears. A miracle. We watched the baby whale exit its mother's birth canal into the Pacific Ocean. First the tail. Then the head. Within minutes, mom and calf slipped away and the water was still. With tears running down our cheeks, we sat in reverent silence.

Another gift from God.

Dolphin Light

BY PAULA TIMPSON

I just knew I had to go to Bermuda. It was a deep calling. Something special would happen. I could feel it deep down inside. Swimming with the dolphins had always been a childhood dream. One day, when Spirit gave me the wisdom how to do this, I followed it with my whole heart and soul.

We went in mid-June. The weather was ideal, as were our spirits! I was excited as a little girl when the morning to take my dolphin swim came. I felt free and openhearted as ever! My husband proudly watched as I swam and played with my dolphin friend. I felt true joy in the moment, which seemed to last forever, yet it was timeless and forever a part of us. As the dolphin laughed and fluttered his body in the shiny water, I, too, was filled with so much light and hope.

We had been playing with the idea of having a child. After my dolphin swim, I felt open and ready. Right after I finished swimming, it rained, and I felt that the water pouring down upon us was a baptism. I let go and let God work with me — within me.

The dolphin led me to have the courage to be a mother and trust that whatever God wanted was truly best. We tried later in the summer, and I got pregnant easily. My son is pure love. Jamesey is our miracle! He makes us better people, stronger and more aware of life as it is. I believe the shining light near Jamesey's heart was carried over by my dolphin friend.

Sometimes, only pure Spirit knows what we need to be happy, and when we find the answer quietly within, we must follow. Only then do we become who we are really meant to be. It was a true gift to have this opportunity! Thanks be to God.

I Corinthians 13:4: Love is always supportive, loyal, hopeful, and trusting. Love never fails....

The Man of My Dreams

BY CATE PERRY

In 1988, I was your typical fifteen-year-old girl. My priorities had gone from childish games to clothes and boys and…well, a new variety of childish games, I suppose. Life as a high school freshman was about attaining popularity at almost any cost. My personal attempts included wearing ultra-tight jeans, spraying my bangs up into a virtual wall of hair, and shunning anything that had to do with actually learning. All of this seems like a healthy dose of teenage narcissism, I'm sure, except for the fact that I was willing to starve myself for the attention of a certain boy.

As it turned out, the "Power That Is" had a different boy in mind for me, and although everything about him was the last thing I'd ever expected, he had more of an impact on my life than I'd ever thought possible.

Take, for example, that this boy was not born yet — androgynous to us at the time, simply referred to as "the baby." Even at that microscopic size, the baby added a new perspective to my life and gave me something to look forward to that was completely separate from my own ego. As he grew through the months, I got to feel him kick within my mother's womb. And, eventually, his due date came and went — and receded through the weeks, three to be exact.

I was shrinking from sight as well, using both anorexia and bulimia to achieve my ultimate goal of reaching 115 pounds. For a five-foot-seven, fifteen-year-old girl, this wasn't exactly realistic — nor was the idea that this kind of self-punishment could somehow result in true love.

At any rate, my brother's birthday was supposed to be June 4. However, it wasn't until June 27 that the doctors induced labor for the third time. My mother was bleeding internally, the baby was in an agitated state, and they would need to perform an emergency C-section, stat. I left my extended family in the waiting room to go outside and have it out with God.

That's right; I told him I didn't believe in him anymore.

Even when I finally held my brother in my arms for the first time, I reminded God I didn't believe in him.

And as I helped bathe my baby brother and feed him and found myself in love with someone who would never use me or hurt me, I reminded God I didn't believe in him.

Needless to say, one day it occurred to my adolescent mind that if I didn't believe in God, then who the heck was I praying to?

And didn't my mom make it out of surgery just fine?

Wasn't my brother perfect?

Didn't God go on to allow my brother to teach me what was truly important in life, down to this very day? That the amount I weighed would have nothing to do with attaining God's grace?

Yes, I was granted a miracle in my brother, and I know just who to thank for it.

Miracle Memo

My wife is a miracle, too. She was diagnosed with multiple sclerosis about fifty years ago, and it is a problem in some ways today, but what people predicted would happen never did. One of the reasons was her four pregnancies and five children born during the seven years following her diagnosis. Today we use some of the same hormones that increase during pregnancy to treat MS; they quiet the body's immune system so it does not attack the fetus, and then the mother benefits further as her autoimmune disease is treated by them, too. It is similar to what cortisone does to reduce inflammation. So it is a built-in miracle available to us all.

What Tanya Chernov shares about Rachel's experience is a miracle; indeed, we are created as miracles and our potential is miraculous. If bacteria and viruses can alter their genes to resist antibiotics and vaccines, and plants can do it to resist diseases and climate changes, then we can, too.

I am sure that Linnea's presence in the hospital also changed Rachel's chemistry, and her body responded to the peace and love her baby brought her. I have seen this many times in the ICU when pets are brought in to say good-bye and the patient's condition improves and they survive or when a mother was allowed to hold her dying premature infant and it started suckling and survived.

As Tanya says, doubts and fears do not help, but

they are often what we sense in family, while love and support help us to heal. Children and animals do that naturally. The visits of loved ones help us to heal and feel less pain.

Dolphins are intuitive and can sense what is going on in our lives and bodies. Often I hear of the profound impressions they make upon people who get close to them in the water. I had a patient of mine, Marilyn, go to Florida to die among friends who were therapists and who worked with dolphins. When Marilyn entered the water she said the dolphins knew where her cancer was and were so gentle in how they approached and treated her, and it touched her deeply. Marilyn lived for many more years because of the dolphins. Eventually, when she was ready to die and complaining about the process, I told her, "I've never had a dolphin complain about it." She died quietly that night.

Dolphins sense human needs and help people recover. I have even heard of dolphins helping people with paralyzing injuries by moving their affected limbs. I would say they sensed Paula Timpson's resistance to having a child and communicated a new feeling to her. I think this was group therapy for Paula. She found the courage she needed to move toward her joy and personal miracle. If you want wonderful things to happen in your life, do what Paula did: jump in and immerse yourself in the nature of life.

Water is itself a miracle; it plays a role in every religion. It can change from vapor to liquid to solid depending on the circumstances and is a role model for us all. We have the potential to change, too, and overcome our droughts or floods. It also shows miracles are built into the system — water being the only liquid that when frozen becomes less dense, lighter, and able to float, thus preserving life on this planet. All those wonderful creatures of the water, including the whales Christie Gorsline mentions, would die if the lakes and oceans froze from the bottom up. Instead they are protected by ice every winter.

In itself, it was a miracle for Christie and Rick to have spent three years cruising the coast of Mexico.

Cate Perry talks about control, but there is only one thing we can control: our thoughts. On the other hand, in an unhealthy way, we can try to control things, such as our eating habits and weight, in order to feel empowered. When things are eating away at us, we can become addicted to food, drugs, and alcohol as a way of numbing the pain and making us feel good in an unhealthy way, which really cannot compete with what love brings us.

Sometimes what seems like a loss of faith can become a blessing. The experiences that made Cate not believe in God also led her to the gift she did receive and her gratitude to God. We all need to be willing to look for the blessing in the problem, to take the darkness or charcoal of life and, under pressure, turn it into a diamond.

Let your legacy live
through all of your creations.

CHAPTER TWO

Animal Inspiration

Until one has loved an animal, a part of one's soul remains unawakened.

—Anatole France

A nimals are wonderful role models for all of us. As a child whose dog was about to be euthanized said, "Animals have shorter lives, because they don't need all the time we do to learn about love and forgiveness."

A while back, we rescued a dog and named him Furphy. After a few days, he attacked our rabbit Smudge, and we were all very upset. Two weeks later I went out in the yard to bring Smudge into the house. She didn't want to come in, so she ran and hid behind Furphy. I was very impressed by her ability to forgive.

Another thing animals do is accept themselves and us as we are. They do not look and see what is wrong or missing from their bodies or ours. They see completeness and our essence. A veterinarian I know once told me how the animals she operated on helped her to get through her mastectomy: "They wake up and lick their owners' faces. They know they are here to love and be loved and teach us a few things."

We need to learn from animals and all of life and create a world filled with love, forgiveness, and compassion. When I watch videos of mother pigs nursing tiger cubs and of an elephant petting a dog's stomach with his massive limb, I am impressed by the true nature of life displayed by God's complete creations.

What follows is a series of stories that speak to the infinite ways animals become blessings and inspire us. These stories show how people's interactions with animals result in rewards for both the giver and receivers of that love.

Not a Sparrow Falls

BY CINDY HURN

I feed wild baby birds: abandoned chicks, orphaned chicks, and sometimes they-just-got-separated-from-their-mother chicks. My back aches after four hours feeding eighty hungry birds. Why do I bother? Because I was hungry, orphaned, and separated-from-mother. Why birds? Because they fly. Because, like God, they are ubiquitous — always there, no matter where I go. They teach me. I can't imagine life without birds.

A young jay escapes his basket cage to make his first clumsy flight indoors. As he swoops over my head, I reach up, fingers outstretched, and catch him. Wild bird in my hand, his heart throbs against my palm; warm talons grip my finger, eye of intelligence stares back at me, offended — caught — yet determined to fly again.

At the wildlife sanctuary, I take the first shift on a Saturday morning. Without food all night, the chicks are hungry and they're vulnerable. If they don't get protein and liquid every twenty to forty minutes, some will die. As I walk into the room, it explodes with heart-piercing cries.

I begin with the incubator chicks. Hours old, they have no feathers. Their skin is waxy and translucent, giving them the look of lizards. I pick up the first infant. His bottom is distended. I reach for the olive oil beside the incubator and place one small drop on my middle finger. Ever so gently I lubricate the skin around his anus. Next, I take a clean eyedropper and tap the side of the chick's beak. Reflex opens his mouth. In relation to his body, the open mouth is enormous. I squeeze the dropper: one, two, three, waiting between each drop for the ugly little creature to swallow.

Next I scoop a small lump of protein mash onto the end of a feeding stick. The monster mouth senses what is coming and opens so wide I fear it will become unhinged. I aim the mash deep in the side of the throat. The mouth clamps down on the stick, revealing the chick's head. It jabs in greedy motions, trying to swallow the whole stick. I hang on to it, surprised at the chick's strength. Beneath his jaw, a dark bulge forms in his crop, a pouch-like pocket hidden in his throat where food slowly digests as the chick waits for its mother's return.

After gulping three scoops of mash, the monster mouth remains shut and the chick's bottom takes over, thrusting upward. The anus gathers into a knot, like pursed lips preparing to blow. A milk-white bubble of gel emerges, slips out of the opening, and plops onto a paper towel below. I glow with pride at this constipated child of wild who manages to poop. His bulging eyes drop heavy lids. His head wobbles then flops to rest on my finger. In my hand, a day-old wild chick sleeps. I pause to wonder at the miracle of life. Urgent squeals remind me of my task, so I place the sleeping infant in a clean tissue nest and reach for the second of this four-sibling family.

One morning, as I sit beside the incubator, I could swear I hear, at the far end of the room, a soft laugh, followed by another voice saying, "Hello." It sounds like my voice. I turn toward the direction of the laugh, but no one is there. The only other person in the room, the sanctuary shift manager, stands beside me.

"Did you hear that?" I ask. "I thought I heard someone laughing."

"It's that blue jay down at the end," she chuckles. "He mimics our voices. He's been spooking the volunteers all week long."

When I finish feeding the incubator chicks, I move over to baskets in the center of the room. The card on one basket states "Towhees x 2," but only one bird sits on the perch. Perhaps one died, I think. The bird eagerly accepts water, mash, and mealy worms. Normally we give four to six scoops of mash followed by four to five worms. Some birds, like finches, will eat until they are sick, but the towhee, when satiated, refuses food.

On accepting the fifth worm, the towhee doesn't swallow. He grips it in the middle, as it wiggles and squirms from both sides of his beak. One large eye stares back at me; his head tilts, as if asking me a question. I need to move on to the next basket, but I could swear he is trying to communicate. I wait. Suddenly, he turns and hops into the far corner, where the net covering has twisted into a roll. Grasping onto the wall of the basket, he reaches out and thrusts the worm toward the net. A beak emerges from the roll, and the towhee stuffs the worm down its throat.

Oh my God, there's another bird in the basket!

I untangle the material to free the trapped towhee, whose foot is caught in a small tear in the netting. Too weak to perch, he squats on the floor of the basket. Smaller than the first towhee, he only accepts two drops of water, but wolfs down the mash with gusto. When I offer a worm, it is so lively I can't get it into the small bird's throat quickly enough. The worm heaves itself out of the open mouth and squiggles across the basket floor. Immediately the bigger towhee hops down and snatches up the worm. At first I think he's stealing it, but he turns and feeds it to the smaller bird. I offer three more worms. Accepting each one, he then turns to feed his smaller companion. His action probably saves that little bird's life.

The realization of what I have witnessed fills my heart with wonder, confirming God's care for us and for all creatures. Tears welling up, I tell the shift manager what just happened. She smiles but doesn't seem surprised. They often take care of each other, she says. Even so, for me, this moment is a miracle.

Blind Faith

BY PAULA TIMPSON

Little did my husband, Jimmy, and I know how much we would learn from our adopted American white Eskimo dog, Fritz. We called him "The White Angel." Love came through his heart into ours. Spirit knew we needed him, so he came to us easily and simply!

Fritz was a miracle. His fur shined rainbows. He danced on the big ocean waves, even when he was blind in his later years. Fritz was always with us, and he lived a full life, enjoying sushi, traveling to Florida, and meeting many special friends. He helped the elderly smile at the nursing home as a pet therapy dog.

Fritz walked by faith, not by sight. His heart led him to where he had to go, and his keen sense of smell helped him live a good life. He always saw with his heart, and now more than ever before, he showed us how to trust life. The scent of deer was always present to dear Fritz, who adored peaceful East Hampton, Long Island, living. The sea lovingly held blind Fritz up so he could float freely in pure joy, as if he were riding a surfboard! Fritz's bravery ignited within us a Spirit of Belief, of miracles and of open hearts! How capable he was — never pitying himself, but truly coping.

Fritz was a strong, beautiful soul, always protecting us and playing tricks. Once in Florida, Fritz disappeared. He was nowhere to be seen, as I searched around for him near the beach. I went back upstairs and found him there already, waiting for me. He had quietly, wisely taken the elevator back up, all by himself.

As he grew older, he remained very independent, even though his eyesight failed. Fritz opened the door with his nose and made his way down the stairs to go out to the bathroom. He circled around to come back in. Watching Fritz circle around, independent, yet dependent on God, I found that pure faith led him to find his way. He taught us all true courage and hope. Fritz was a strong, beautiful soul, always protecting me and playing tricks with Jimmy. He knew how to "be" peace and love. Finally, Fritz became really weak and life became a struggle and no longer fun for him. I watched my husband gaze at his beloved dog. I prayed he would have the courage to let him go.

I reflected on sea memories, Fritz's laughter, and all the little jokes he played as I watched Jimmy touch Fritz on the top of his head, Jimmy's eyes tender and loving, full of tears. I knew inside my heart, Jimmy was courageously saying good-bye to his dear friend. When his spirit left his body, Fritz's soft smile created freedom for my husband and me. As my husband and I stood side by side, we felt and watched his soul fly to heaven. There was a tiny smile on Fritz's face as he left this world, although he remains here, always the pure, loving spirit that he is. It was a moment we both will never forget. The miracle was that when we threw Fritz's ashes into the ocean, we trusted life fully. We saw the dream of letting go and the reality of believing.

Fritz already showed us how much love we had within, if we opened our hearts to trust life. When we spread Fritz's ashes into the windy ocean, our hearts rushed out to sea to be with his beautiful soul. It was miraculous as we saw the reality of letting go and the dream of believing in life.

Fritz was with us since our beginnings; he grew with us and watched us to the end, always loving. Blind Fritz was Blind Faith and is now forever free.

Ricochet the Dog

BY JUDY FRIDONO

Ricochet was slated to be a service dog, but she had to be released from that role due to her instinct to chase birds and other small animals, which could be a risk to a person with a disability. I still wanted her to do something meaningful with her life, and rather than focus on what she couldn't do, I focused on what she *could* do, and that was surfing. So, she went from service dog to *surf*ice dog and began surfing for charitable causes.

But once I let go of who I wanted Ricochet to be, and just let her "be," the miracles began and amazing things happened! Her first miracle was for a quadriplegic boy, and through sponsorship, she raised over $10,000 for his rehab therapy. Because of her unique and highly skilled background of service/therapy/surf dog training, Ricochet surfs with disabled surfers and special-needs kids for therapeutic purposes, perhaps the only dog in the world who does. One of her sponsors awarded a grant to cover an additional three years of the young boy's therapy. This boy is an adaptive surfer, and Ricochet tandem-surfs with him, helping to counterbalance the board, which keeps it from tipping in the waves. The biggest miracle of this story is a video that shows the boy walking.

Surfing isn't the only thing Ricochet does to raise money. In fact, if she never got on a surfboard again, it would not affect her success in raising awareness and money. She has even raised money while being injured. For example, we held a toy drive featuring Ricochet at Christmas and raised over $3,500, which bought toys for 630 children in two hospitals and two women's shelters. The children (and parents) viewed this as a miracle!

Ricochet then turned her miracle-producing spirit on a six-year-old boy who suffered a severe brain injury in a horrific car accident that claimed the lives of his parents. She has helped to raise thousands for the boy thus far.

Ricochet also donated a year's supply of dog food to a local animal shelter, and when the founders of the "Pay It Forward" organization heard about Ricochet's far-reaching acts of kindness, inspiration, and miracle work, they asked her to become their ambassador. Ricochet has over sixteen thousand fans from all over the world, including places like Japan, the Netherlands, the Bahamas, Switzerland, France, China, and more, who are inspired by her miracles and read updates about her and respond with generosity.

Ricochet demonstrates miracles that can be applied to anyone and anything. People from all walks of life are enriched and inspired by the message of adjusting expectations and focusing on ability, which allows for a celebration of amazing miracles. Many teachers have used Ricochet's journey as a source of inspiration for their students. Women's prisons are using it for their inmates, life coaches incorporate it for their clients' goals, and many others are using her story to showcase miracles in action and demonstrate that lives can be changed.

I had wanted Ricochet to make a difference in one person's life, but she had other plans. Instead, she is touching millions with her miracles and changing lives in the process. Ricochet is just an ordinary dog with an extraordinary spirit who exemplifies the notion that miracles do happen! She has increased my sense of gratitude beyond words, and this entire journey has been so emotionally overwhelming (in a good way) that I have never felt so connected to the divine.

The Child Whisperer

BY MARY ROSE ANDERSON

The message about a stray cat was on my machine when we came home from our daughter's open-heart surgery. A thirty-something single mother, I was focused on the success of the surgery and didn't think much of it. "Now everything will go much better for us" was the thought replaying in my head. I couldn't have been more wrong. Getting my eleven-year-old's heart fixed was the easy part.

Frances had always been a high-maintenance child with behavior problems, mood disorders, and learning disabilities in addition to the congenital heart defect. As I look back to this time in my life, I see a stream of experts helping me care for her. One of those "experts" was exceptional, though not certified, nor — with four legs and a tail — even "credible" to some.

When I had taken Frances to the cognitive and academic specialists for testing, I received a twelve-page report with a devastating seven lines devoted to her multiple diagnoses. The ODD, oppositional defiant disorder, made things hardest of all, because Frances would go into temper tantrums whether she wanted to or not. With enormous blue eyes and a body as skinny and willowy as Olive Oyl's, Frances was as volatile and episodic as Helen Keller in *The Miracle Worker*. Annie Sullivan was the child whisperer for young Helen. Harry the Angel Cat played that role for Frances.

After her heart surgery, I prayed fervently for an answer other than hospitalization, when I suddenly remembered my girlfriend's recent call about a cat who was about to be euthanized at a nearby animal shelter. His temperament was so lovely the secretary at the front desk had actually made a tearful scene objecting to euthanizing him.

I finished my prayer and called the shelter. Thank heavens it wasn't too late.

Harry was a beautiful eighteen-pound male stray. He had fluffy, long gray hair, with a regal white breast. Gorgeous and docile, he quickly became Frances's best friend. Mine, too. Harry was a miracle worker and could motivate Frances to do many a difficult thing.

I had tried time-outs on Frances and they didn't work. Now when Frances acted out, Harry the cat — not Frances — would have to go into time-out. A quarantined cat was more than Frances could bear. She truly tried to behave better in order to get the cat back.

I had a daily rewards system set up for Frances regardless of her behavior. Once a day, we had a twenty-minute period where she got to do anything she wanted — within reason. Habitually, Frances wanted to go on twenty-minute car rides with Harry on her lap!

Harry also went for walks on a leash. He even allowed Frances to seat-belt him into the child carrier seat on the rear wheel of my bicycle. He could have easily escaped the restraints and fled the scene, but he did not. He just rode around the neighborhood with her — to the delight of neighborhood kids.

Frances had trouble making and keeping friends. Harry filled the void. He wore doll clothes and paper hats, slept in a doll rocker, and heroically chased big, scary dogs away from the yard. But most important, he faithfully slept with Frances every night. When Frances was assigned to draw a picture of God at church, she drew a picture of Harry sleeping. He was her image of unconditional love.

Harry attended Frances's tutoring sessions because that's where her behavior problems were often the worst. The tutor was teaching Frances how to work with fractions and decimals, a particularly tough task because of Frances's arithmetic disability. With Harry sitting on top of the study table, Frances worked hard to learn how to calculate decimals — by balancing a checkbook register. When she mastered a problem, she repeated what she'd just learned *to the cat*. Whisking his tail, Harry patiently listened. Very smart cat.

The tutor and Frances also baked pizzas and cut them into fractions. They would shuffle pizza pieces to figure out a problem, and then eat them with Harry's help. The cat loved hamburger on pizza!

Eleven years later, the same math tutor phoned Frances and me from Japan, not knowing Harry was seriously sick. While Harry panted and struggled to breathe, I held the phone up to his ear, and the tutor told her faithful assistant good-bye.

After hanging up the phone, I realized I must say good-bye, too. I whispered to him with the intensity of a prayer: "Thank you for all that you've done for Frances." That moment, Harry let out a long, drawn-out exhale.

If he were human, he'd have been about ninety. He had been waiting for me to tell him his work was done and done well. When I had saved his life over a decade earlier, I hadn't realized that he would reciprocate a hundredfold. And that he'd truly live up to his name.

Miracle Memo

We had a cat named Miracle. She lived to be twenty, and she was truly a miracle, too. She accompanied me on my rounds when I was going to nursing homes and other places to help people. She was named after a cat that appeared in a woman's dream and told her how to treat her cancer. The woman listened and is well today. I may add it is also lots of fun to run around outside your house yelling, "Miracle, Miracle," when you can't find her and watch how it changes your neighbor's reaction to your behavior.

What Cindy Hurn is living and doing, volunteering to help and rescue animals, makes her a very exceptional human being. When people experience rejection, they can end up seeking revenge and being depressed. By caring for birds, Cindy chose to live in love, and her compassion can be felt by us all.

In Paula Timpson's story, Fritz shows us that animals live in the present and are more at peace and forgiving than we are. As Fritz demonstrates, meditating is easier for animals because they are living in the moment and not thinking with words and verbalizing fearful futures or reliving painful wounds. All animals are complete and are wonderful teachers for incomplete human beings like us.

What Ricochet the dog teaches and demonstrates is exactly the path to miracles. Judy Fridono's canine companion shows us how to give up the untrue self and live the life we were meant to. Not only is she on the right path in her life but she has healed many others, too. She is a coach and a shining example. When people spend the time they have left in their lives doing what feels right to them, miracles happen.

Adopting a miracle, as Mary Rose Anderson did, can improve your life in many ways. In fact, study after study shows the benefits of having a furry pet in your home and how it helps improve survival and relationships.

Pets bring joy in so many ways. They help people to bond and demonstrate that we can communicate through our consciousness and do not need words to do so. My wife always asks me who I met after I walk the dogs. She knows what can happen.

If you want to create a miracle,
find the surfboard of your life and get on it!

CHAPTER THREE

Dreams and Symbols

Dreams are today's answers to tomorrow's questions.

— Edgar Cayce

Signs, dream messages, and symbols exist in our conscious and unconscious minds to guide us through the puzzles life can throw our way. These guides have been an integral part of my life, as well as for countless patients.

When I ran my first marathon, to raise funds for the lymphoma and leukemia society, I asked God for a sign that I would finish the twenty-six miles. Pennies are symbolic to me, with their messages of "Liberty" and "In God We Trust," so I thought that if I found twenty-six cents, I would know all was well. Standing in the starting area on Staten Island, with twenty thousand people, I looked down at my feet, and there between them was a quarter. Now all I needed was a penny, and sure enough on a street in Manhattan, there it was. I risked being trampled to stop and pick it up. I could hear people saying, "How poor can he be?" I had my miracle and finished the race and received my medal, and I still have those coins.

A patient I knew had a dream about a white cat. In the dream it told her its name was Miracle and the chemotherapy she needed to take, a question she had been worrying over. She and her doctor followed Miracle's advice, and she was cured. I once had an iridescent white cat appear in one of my dreams. I thought her name was Diamond because of the way she sparkled, but people weren't pronouncing her name correctly. They were leaving off the final *d*. Jungian psychologist James Hillman told me her name is Daimon — and that it represents our inner spirit, the seed we need to grow and become who we were meant to be. He made me aware of that new symbolism, and what she represented was my essence and core being. I think we sleep in order to dream and not only rest.

The white animal is symbolic in many cultures, from the Native American's white buffalo to the Buddhist's white elephant. White to me is like a blank canvas, and we all are in the process of creation. We are works in progress and have the potential to create a work of art using ourselves and our lives by not fearing loss, change, judgment, and failure.

The following writers share some of my favorite

stories about dreams and symbols. For Barbara J. Semple and Terri Elders, winged creatures appeared in their dreams to save their lives, in both literal and figurative senses. Susan Hoffman's dream acted as a premonition to get her on the right track during a time of crisis.

Dolphin Dreams

BY JANET COLLI

I was diagnosed with cancer at the age of thirty. My world was shattered. Within one week of my diagnosis with Hodgkin's, I read an interview with Bernie Siegel, who I knew was the author of a book about healing, *Love, Medicine & Miracles.* In the interview, he spoke about George, his spirit guide whom not everyone can see, and the belief that *disease is a divine message of redirection.* That interview transformed my views about cancer.

One month later, with construction paper and scissors in hand, I pieced together a portrait of Dr. Bernie Siegel, and I left the space to his left *blank* to represent George. Seeing my cancer as a creative challenge — instead of merely a threat — was the beginning of a new life.

For three years after my diagnosis I focused on emotional healing, avoiding allopathic medical treatment. Hodgkin's lymphoma is curable, but I simply did not trust doctors. My fear of nausea cut too close to the bone. After a bout of food poisoning and hospitalization at three years old, I started refusing food. My mother, after all, had emotional problems that focused on food. She ate mostly bananas, cottage cheese, and Milky Way candy bars. My father was a doctor who threatened to give me "shots" when I refused to eat. Little wonder I developed phobias about nausea and needles. *What is chemotherapy but nausea and needles?* Not until I was dying did I choose to face my fears of chemotherapy. That choice ushered in a psycho-spiritual transformation — and it was sparked by a dream.

In the dream, I remember an indoor swimming pool...I remember wandering up to a bulletin board. Tacked to the bulletin board was a notice. The notice announced that Janet Colli would be facilitating dolphin encounters with cancer patients.

I had that dream in the winter of 1987. I was dying.

But dolphins? Not a single dolphin graced my dream. I had no conscious desire to make the connection. Yet suddenly the decision to take chemotherapy and radiation was simple. Bedridden and debilitated, I took comfort in my dreams. But the dream that saved my life was far from dramatic. Its significance was subtle. Pleasant. I awoke refreshed and consoled by its promise; for I took that notice on the bulletin board as assurance that I was meant to live. And that reassurance gave me the courage to fight.

My sheer faith in that dream enabled me to make the long-dreaded decision to initiate allopathic medical treatment. I knew I would survive. And if I were meant to live, I had to do everything in my power — even chemotherapy and radiation. Suddenly it was not such a threat to me.

Others were dreaming for me, too. Like Carol, a facilitator at my support group for life-*challenging* illness. Carol dreamt she was in the passenger seat of a jeep that I was driving. As we fast approached a cliff, a wide chasm opened up before us. Carol despaired of surviving the breach. She turned to face me in the driver's seat — but I had disappeared! In my place sat…the *Water Saint*. Our dream-jeep, piloted by the newly-embodied saint, *shot* across the chasm. We landed safely — on the other side of the abyss. We had miraculously survived.

The key to survival was the transformation of my self-identity — formed by fear of my doctor father — and the engulfment of my ego by the sacred archetype of water. *Feminine fluidity*. Chemotherapy began to symbolize the water element cleansing my cells. Dolphins — embodying bliss beyond ego — were the perfect agents of transformation that had been brought to me in my early dream. I saw my cancer as a call to a deeper level of love. Though I had planned to forgo allopathic medicine and heal through "natural means," my dream of dolphins ushered in a path of spiritualizing Western medicine.

After a half year of a highly toxic chemotherapy regimen — even by chemotherapy standards — I was thriving. But the medical treatment for Hodgkin's was only *half* over. Radiation treatment was about to commence. But how could healing happen in the inner sanctum of the radiation chamber? How was such a death ray to effect healing?

When the machine finally whirred on, I tried to hold my breath, convinced that by shrinking and stilling myself, I would elude some of the rays. I desperately prayed as the machine emitted its invisible, deadly rays.

After that first treatment I knew I had to renew my consecration to Life. It wasn't the treatment that scared me so much as my own attitude toward it. I could not help but perceive the radiation as a deadly affair. And I did not want to face another session without a radical change in that perception.

It had become my touchstone that if I asked for help, Creation would see to it that someone suitable would arrive on the scene. Call it bargaining with God, but time after time, I had experienced the saving grace of surrender. This time was no exception.

I duly considered one of the two female technicians intent upon adjusting my body on the table. I noted a silver crucifix hanging on a delicate chain around her neck. Luckily, she was delegated last contact with me. So I took a calculated risk. When the time came for her to vacate the premises, I made an urgent request.

"Can't you say something…*a little more healing*?"

The young woman dressed in a white coat touched my forehead, marking out a tiny cross.

"Christ be with you," she said.

With her touch lingering and with a full heart, I proceeded with the radiation treatment. But this time when the technicians left the room, I was not alone. Thus my faith was ignited and my healing caught fire.

Henceforth, we ritually dedicated the radiation sessions to the radiant energy of Christ. Putting myself in the Hands of Christ was a cinch. I simply envisioned the job of subsuming cancerous cells and protecting healthy cells and tissues — as being over-seen by Jesus Christ, Chief of Radiation Oncology.

Four years later, my art exhibit, consisting of eighteen pictures and commentary, celebrated the reopening of the Oncology Department of the University of Washington Medical Center; it was displayed several times. In 1989, Bernie saw it displayed at the American Holistic Medical Association conference, and he drew a huge heart in my gallery book.

Thank you, Bernie and George. You helped to save my life. Now, over twenty years later, as a psychotherapist, I believe that symptoms are a communication mechanism. Our total personality seeks above all to express itself. *Your biggest symptom just might be your greatest dream trying to break through.*

The Walker and the Butterfly

BY BARBARA J. SEMPLE

About twelve years ago, I was coping with some of the absolute worst immobilizing pain of rheumatoid arthritis. I felt like I was dying and was pretty sure that was the truth.

The Shinto religion says that every human is a little *kami,* a Japanese word meaning noble, sacred spirit. So I am a noble, sacred spirit, and I have had a very difficult time accepting that, because rheumatoid arthritis had caused severe swelling in my feet, hands, and joints — to the extent that I could not bend my knees, and I needed to use a walker. I said I was too young — only forty-four years old. I didn't want to look like all the elderly folks using walkers. A walker was another, more visible sign that I had lost more control over my life.

One day, all I could do was surrender to the help the walker would give me. After I surrendered again, the gifts came. Gratitude…the walker helped me keep my joints stable, slowing down degeneration. It gave me more mobility to get around safely and has even corrected my posture. I admit it. The walker has been helpful. And I can carry stuff on it, too. I have made peace with the walker. It is an act of self-love for me to keep myself comfortable through illness.

There were days I was experiencing a great deal of discomfort. I felt overwhelmed by the physical struggle. One morning I had just finished yelling to (not at) my husband, and to "whoever" would hear me, that I hated my body and I hated the arthritis. I was not feeling very whole or holy. My husband gave me some Jin Shin Jyutsu hands-on support, and I fell back to sleep. I had a marvelous dream.

In my dream, I was looking at my walker. It is one of those steel or aluminum things, which has special armrests for me. A pretty accessory it is not. The walker was next to my bed, so it was close to my eye level. In my dream I was lying down. I then sat up, and I noticed something wriggle out from under one of the clamps of the walker, which adjusts the height of the walker. The wriggly thing positioned itself in front of the walker. I saw a pure white insect with white antennae and front legs, and it rolled like a burrito, opened its wings, and became a giant white butterfly. Then as I sat on the bed, in my dream, two white butterflies came out of the palms of my hands!

Something deeply spiritual continues to remind me to keep going. That out of the most rigid physical circumstance comes the purest butterfly, and the confinement and condition symbolized by the walker is actually a cocoon for the butterfly, symbolic of a transmutation to pure, light, fluid motion.

Even now, I am experiencing outstanding soul movement, and still I am dealing with a debilitating physical condition. I wonder if my life has value, especially times when I feel tired, hungry, or overwhelmed by the medicines I am taking. And then I receive such a wonderful message from Soul, and I am reminded of my true self again. My spiritual life is so rich. There is that element of unknowing, of the Great Mystery of life. I accept that. I simply know in my heart that I am more than my physical body and its circumstances. That keeps me going forward with Spirit.

Today I do not need a walker and have not used one for twelve years. You can find me, among other physically active options, playing Nintendo Wii doubles tennis with my husband, doing water aerobics, hiking, gardening, and so on.

Bats in Our Belfry

BY TERRI ELDERS

One of my favorite quotes is by James Russell Lowell, and it reads: *All God's angels come to us disguised.*

Recently I visited Scotts Mills, Oregon, and gazed at the Victorian house on the crest of the hill at Sixth and Grandview. It still stands, one of the few remaining homes from the little town's 1890s heyday. Decades ago I'd lived there with my grandparents, parents, sister, and brother, and a colony of bats…or a host of angels, depending on your perspective.

When my family moved there from Southern California right at the close of World War II, I appropriated the unfinished storage room at the end of the second-story hallway as my playroom. I propped my dolls atop the cardboard boxes that lined the walls and tried to teach them to read. When I'd tire of their stubborn lack of cooperation, I'd curl up on a cot and read to myself.

Late one warm afternoon I drifted to sleep over *Hans Brinker.* I remember I'd been dreaming I was Gretel, skating down the canal alongside my brother, pacing my glides to the muffled squeals in the background that sounded like little kisses. Then something soft and silky caressed my cheek. I opened my eyes to see a cloud of bats circle overhead and then flutter out the open window.

I suspect I shrieked loud enough for folks to hear

me down at the general store, a good quarter mile away. I heard footsteps pounding down the hall, and Grandma and Mama burst into the room.

"Bats!" I declared, pointing toward the window. "There were bunches of them. They woke me up."

Grandma perched on the cot next to me. "Are you certain?"

"Yes! I saw at least four or five. One of them touched me."

"Well, they didn't hurt you, so come down for supper. There's macaroni and cheese, and apple pie for dessert."

That evening I asked Mama if I could say we had bats in our belfry.

"No," Mama said, chuckling. "We don't have a belfry, just an attic. A belfry is a bell tower, like at the Friends Church."

Well, close enough, I thought, making a mental note to confer with my Sunday school teacher. That Sunday I cornered Miss Magee and asked if the church had bats in the belfry. She always took our questions seriously, unlike some adults, but nonetheless I could see her struggling to hide a smile. I wondered what was so funny. I thought bats were more scary than amusing.

"They do flit around the bell tower at night," she said. "And we have them in most of the old houses. But don't be scared of bats. They're helpful. They eat insects, clean their fur like cats, and protect farmers against rootworm. We should be grateful for them, just as we are for so many of God's creatures."

I was glad I'd asked. Miss Magee knew just about everything. Now I looked forward to seeing them again, but the bats avoided the storage room the rest of the summer.

Then one nippy autumn night, tucked safely in bed, I dreamed once again of that strange chirpy chatter that sounded like baby kisses.

"Wake up, Terri," a tinkling voice whispered.

I opened my eyes but had to squint against the sting of smoke. Coughing, I scrambled to the window to let air into the room. Through the thick gray haze I caught a glimpse of two or three tiny silvery winged shapes wafting out the window into the night. Must be bats, I thought, and stumbled into the hallway.

"The house is on fire!" I screamed. Everybody, including my brother and sister, rushed from their bedrooms into the hall and thundered down the stairs, gagging and hacking.

"Look! It's the particleboard that's caught fire!" Daddy yelled. He and Grandpa grabbed some bathroom towels, soaked them in the sink, and slapped them against the walls on either side of the fireplace. Grandma and Mama scurried from room to room, throwing open all the downstairs windows to let smoke escape.

"It must have been the bats that woke me up," I announced, once we were certain that our house wouldn't be the latest Victorian to go up in flames. Another house had burned down just a few weeks earlier, the second that year.

"Bats?" Mama asked, wrinkling her brow.

"I heard them in my dream. They called my name …and told me to wake up."

"They must have been looking for an escape from the house," Grandpa said, giving me a strange look. "But how did they get into your bedroom? Your door was closed."

"I don't know. But they did."

The next Sunday when I told Miss Magee that bats had saved our house from burning down, she frowned. "Bats? You saw bats?"

"Well, my room was very smoky. But they had wings. And they called my name."

She grinned. "Talking bats?"

"What else could it have been? I'm too old to believe in fairies."

"Just think," Miss Magee said, taking my hand. "Which of God's creatures has wings, can talk, and doesn't need an open door or window to get into a room? Don't you remember what we learned about guardian angels?"

I always could count on Miss Magee to have the answers.

Not long ago somebody asked me if I believed in miracles. Let me tell you…if our old house still stands on the corner of Sixth and Grandview after well over a hundred years, that's a miracle indeed.

And you might think that I have bats in my belfry, but I know that house in Scotts Mills has its own personal guardian angel…maybe even two or three.

The Message

BY SUSAN HOFFMAN

Early one morning in November 1998 I woke up knowing I had breast cancer. I knew exactly where it was,
the exact spot. I'd dreamed I was on a gurney with
about six doctors standing around me. My vision
from the table would only allow me to see their blue
scrubs; I could not see their heads. I knew they were
talking about me, and I strained to hear what they
were saying. Just then, a small-framed woman with
slender fingers touched the top of my right breast.
She said, "The cancer is right here," and then they all
left the room. Because of her delicate hands and skin
tone, I assumed she was Asian.

I immediately woke up, touched my breast where
she had, and felt a rather large lump. I woke my husband and, touching my breast, announced, "I have
breast cancer and it's right here." Needless to say, he
was a bit perplexed and probably thought he was
dreaming.

Was this dream a message from God? Was it a
message from my deceased mother, who had passed
away after her battle with breast cancer? Possibly.
Although I know ultimately the information came
from God, I felt the message came from me. I believed,
as I do even more so today, we know exactly what
our health issues are. If only we knew how to access
this information. Apparently my brain delivered the

message in a way it knew I would have no choice but to pay attention to.

During the next few months I learned to listen to my intuition and to trust my thoughts. A series of miracles happened after the initial dream.

On my way home from UCLA, after having an ultrasound to confirm the fact it most likely was cancer, I was trying to absorb everything. I began to cry some, pray some, and talked to myself a lot. "Okay," I said, "let's do the best-case worst-case scenario. Best case you'll be fine, worst case you'll die." Just then all five lanes of traffic suddenly stopped. As I looked up at the car directly in front of me, through my blurry eyes I noticed the vanity plate read SURVIVR! (I've seen several since, but eleven years ago this was rare.) *Wow.* Was this a coincidence or a message for me? A message, I was sure of it!

Sometime later, during a full day at UCLA — meeting with different doctors who were reviewing each new patient's pathology results, examining us, and ultimately coming up with a treatment plan for us — I was put into a room in which the doctors would come in and feel the tumor site. When they left and I started to get dressed, a female Asian doctor, just like in my dream, came rushing in saying she was in a hurry to get to surgery, touched my breast, and said, "Oh yeah, it's right there, the cancer's right there." This was the hand from my dream!

As I researched my case and read books that seemed to jump off the shelves at the bookstores, I was able to follow my instincts and do what I felt was best for me regardless of the pressure I felt from the medical community and also from family and friends. I chose a combination of allopathic and alternative treatment.

At one point during the next eleven years I read Dr. Siegel's book — *Love, Medicine & Miracles* — and it confirmed that I had chosen the right treatment plan. What I chose came from research and a strong intuition followed by a great sense of a weight being lifted from me. This is when I knew it was the right decision. I decided against chemotherapy because I was so tormented trying to convince myself I should do it.

Now, I am healthy. As a result of my experience, life is no longer a challenge. I know what decisions are right for me, and I have no reason to question myself. What a relief!

Miracle Memo

Doctors are not told that Carl Jung interpreted a dream and diagnosed a brain tumor. Perhaps if we were, we would ask our patients what they had dreamt about their bodies and medical problems.

Years ago, when I experienced bloody urine, I was told in a dream that I did not have cancer. In the dream I was sitting in our cancer support group, and we were introducing ourselves. When it was my turn, before I could say anything, everyone said, "But you don't have cancer."

I also learned to listen to my patients and perform a biopsy or further testing when they told me, even though their mammogram was normal, they knew there was something wrong from their intuition or a dream.

I like to have people become "respants," or responsible participants, and not submissive, suffering good patients who do whatever the doctor tells them and die on schedule. This also includes making your own decisions about treatment and not just filling prescriptions from others. The mind is a powerful tool, and what we believe is communicated to our bodies. So when you believe you are being radiated, your body and tumor respond as if you are, and when chemotherapy is considered the devil giving you poison, versus a gift from God, guess who does well with no side effects?

What Janet Colli is able to do is be empowered.

Not many people are willing to become empowered and participate in their health and life, since if they take responsibility and don't do well, they experience guilt, shame, and blame. Janet is able to love herself and not see the disease as some form of punishment but as growth gone wrong in her body and life; she is able to see her health as something lost, which she seeks to find again. So the cancer becomes God's path to a deeper level of love. The fears and symptoms of her childhood were transcended and led to her healing. That someone is capable of doing this is a miracle.

Barbara Semple realized that her wholeness and true self are not related to the fact she needs a walker. When we lose body parts or need assistance, we can still be whole. She realized that the changes she found difficult caused other changes that benefited her and taught her about life and who she truly is. The symbol of the white butterfly came to her in her dream as a spiritual helper and a symbol of transformation.

A key word Barbara uses is surrender. That does not mean giving up, but it does mean the end of struggling to fix and cure and change. When you surrender, you find peace and learn from your troubles. Nietzsche said, "Love your fate." For me, surrender is defined by the words of Lao-Tzu, which I have on my kitchen wall: "Rejoice in the way things are, be content with what you have, and when you realize nothing is lacking, the whole world belongs to you." That can bring you peace and healing no matter what your life experience may be.

Susan Hoffman's message about the diagnosis in her dream is so full of important wisdom that I could write a book based upon all it contains. First of all, I feel the primary reason we sleep is to be in touch with this inner wisdom. The body cannot talk, but it can communicate through dreams. Sleep lets us do this because then the mind is quiet like a still pond. When the turbulent thinking mind is asleep, the truth can be seen in the reflection of the still water.

Susan also kept her power and chose to do what felt right for her to do. It was not related to not dying, but to doing what she felt was right for her. Then she could live with whatever the future brought. Most important, she changed her life. Now her body gets the message that she loves her life and her body, and it does all it can to help her survive and thrive.

I do a lot of work with drawing by asking people to draw their treatment, disease, and more. Survival behavior is related to rebirthing yourself and to seeing your disease not as blame, guilt, or God punishing you but as a gift, a wake-up call, and a new beginning. I even tell people to pick a new name and create a new life by becoming their authentic selves, rather than losing their life by living the life imposed upon them by various authority figures. When you lose the untrue self and let it die, you save your true and authentic self and rebirth it and your life.

As Terri Elders did, you can see the messengers, or hear them as I often do, and know that God loves you and sends angels in many forms to awaken us and guide us on the path we are meant to live. But you have to be ready and willing to see and listen and not question the message because your intellect will not stop thinking.

When you are happy with your life
the way it is now, the whole
world belongs to you.

CHAPTER FOUR

Miracle Healings

Impossible situations can become possible miracles.

— *Robert H. Schuller*

*O*ur body loves us, but it needs to know we love our lives in order for it to do all it can to help us survive. The change in body energy activated by the love alters our internal chemistry and makes a difference. In many cases, this kind of miracle is damn hard work. But when you are willing to do the work, and live in your heart, magic can happen.

Fear and love play a major role in all our lives. Fear is meant to protect us from danger, not make us ill. Fear can get you to run faster and escape a rabid animal, but if you live in fear of everything and everyone, it will intensify stress and negatively affect your ability to heal. Love and laughter are what enhance healing, reduce stress, and increase our ability to heal. So let your heart make up your mind.

It is important to follow your faith and make choices based upon what you have faith in. That can include yourself, your God, your doctor, your treatments, and more. It's not just doing what others prescribe for you, because when you do that, you give up your power. Every treatment has its side effects, but if you choose a treatment out of faith, the side effects are diminished and the treatment more beneficial. What the mind believes has a very powerful effect on the body.

I have seen innumerable cases of "miracle healings" in my life and practice. Here are a few stories that have inspired me.

Keeping the Tigers in Their Cages

BY BOB ELLAL

In 1991 I was diagnosed with stage-four lymphoma cancer and given six months to live. I was thirty-two. My sons were infants. My ex-wife and I had just built a huge house on a lake. I had everything to live for. Death was not in my plans.

I decided I was going to live to see my sons grow up into men — that I would beat this disease, not just for me, but for them, too. So I researched everything I could about patients who had survived terminal illnesses. A common thread emerged: meditation and visualization. Survivors utilized the mind/body connection to bolster their immune systems. I devoured the books by Dr. Bernie Siegel, which emphasized the vital importance of using the mind to help heal the body.

For the next six months while undergoing chemotherapy, I meditated and visualized five or six times a day. And against all odds, half a year later I was cancer free. I thought I was cured.

About a year later the cancer relapsed, and the doctors recommended a stem cell transplant. It's a risky procedure, with a high mortality rate. I continued meditating, and it helped, since I got out of the transplant room in record time and cancer free.

End of story, right?

A year later the cancer returned, and the oncologists recommended another stem cell transplant. To subject myself to another could mean death from the chemotherapy. The doctors gave me a 20 percent chance of survival.

So I went deeper into the mind/body connection. I learned the secrets of qigong — Chinese internal energy exercises — from a kung fu master. Specifically, standing post meditation: holding a posture, focusing on deep abdominal breathing, and meditating for an hour.

I put in hundreds of hours of qigong in the months preceding my transplant. And it paid off. Once again, I came out in record time (which amazed the doctors — I should have been deathly ill because of my previous transplant) and cancer free.

Then I made a big mistake — I stopped training. I thought I was cured.

My oncologists were at a loss, as I'd already had every type of chemo available to fight lymphoma and had miraculous cures three times. Out of desperation they gave me one round of the original chemo. I practiced standing postures for an hour, twice a day.

In a month the pain was gone, and so was the cancer. That was over fourteen years ago, and I've been cancer free ever since. My son Geoff is now twenty-two and recently returned from a Special Forces tour of duty in the Middle East. He is still, thankfully, in one piece. My younger son, Dylan, age twenty, has just completed several semesters at the New England Institute of Art. My sons have grown into men. I kept my promise.

I still practice qigong every day to keep the tigers

in their cages. I believe daily practice has somehow helped my immune system keep the cancer at bay — or perhaps helped eliminate it. It has also helped me mentally and emotionally...No one walks away from the high-dose chemo of two bone marrow transplants without damage. Daily meditative practice has helped me deal with the pain to my psyche as well as the horrendous damage the cancer inflicted to my skeleton.

"Keeping the tigers in their cages" is my own metaphor. Qigong, and the kung fu systems it's associated with, often use the "tiger" as a metaphor for strength and power (as in, Tiger Claw and Tiger/Crane kung fu). I used some of the qigong from these styles in my recovery and still practice them today. I see the forces working within me on the physical, mental, and emotional planes as strong, indeed — especially during my six-year struggle.

As to losing everything valued in Western society: career, marriage, wealth, house, and so on — in the final analysis, this life experience has helped me reevaluate what is really important.

Be a Good One

BY NATALIE PALMER

My story begins with a quote by Abraham Lincoln, with whom I share a birthday: "Whatever you are, be a good one." Many years ago this became the mission statement of my life and remains so to this day.

I was a person with metastatic cancer who made a promise to be the best person with cancer I could possibly be...I was determined to "be a good one."

My cancer story began with a large lump in my right breast, which after a mammogram and ultrasound I was told was "nothing." Well, this "nothing" hurt like hell, waking me up at night. The pain was comforting because I'd read somewhere that breast cancer didn't hurt, so I had nothing to worry about, right? Wrong! It was cancer.

My reaction, like most people's, was one of disbelief, sadness, fear, anger, and a supreme sense of betrayal; my response was one of grief. I felt sad about what at the time I thought was my imminent death — snubbed out in the prime of life. I was mad at God and the world for this injustice. Hadn't I been a good person?! I was scared out of my wits and felt betrayed by my body.

A million miracles both big and small happened before and during my cancer diagnosis. The right people were placed in my life at the right time over and over again. The right decisions were ultimately made, even if at first they appeared to be the wrong decisions. One example occurred when I visited my primary care provider for my annual exam. She didn't like the "nothing" lump, so I agreed to get another mammogram at a different radiology center. The radiologist reading this mammogram was excellent. In the new mammogram, the docs discovered something was amiss that warranted further investigating, and they were right.

My next miracle occurred during a shower a week after my diagnosis. I was sobbing uncontrollably, doubled over, my whole being in pain, when suddenly the most incredible feeling of pure peace, unconditional love, and calmness washed over me, and a voice said, "You will be okay." It was amazing, and just like that, my pain was gone. The sense was one of the most awesome experiences of love, acceptance, and peace I have ever known.

A week later at 4:30 AM, the same voice, accompanied by a similar sense of supreme love and well-being, said, "Embrace the cancer as a gift from God."

This is how my journey back to myself, back to health, and back to well-being began...in a way I'd never imagined. From that point on I became "a good one" — a good person with cancer, the best I could be. I developed an attitude of thankfulness. I embraced a vegan lifestyle and took supplements. I meditated daily with Dr. Bernie Siegel and Marianne Williamson. I focused on hope and completely felt the depths of my emotions. I let go, forgave others, and most importantly forgave myself. I loved. I laughed. I connected with nature. My life became a prayer. Using a truly integrative approach to cancer, I became what we refer to as a "survivor," and the miracles continue.

My spiritual guides, voices, angels, God — whatever you choose to call them — continue to be a welcome presence in my life during both times of stress and great joy. The biggest miracle has been my ongoing transformation to being "a good one"... *without cancer*. So remember, "Whatever you are, be a good one."

Cancer Survivor

BY MARILYN BECKER GILLIOM

In 1970, I was diagnosed with cancer, and the only treatment at that time was surgery. I had three young children and didn't want to leave them. I prayed for God's intervention and attended healing seminars.

Then in July of 1981, my husband left the marriage for a much younger woman. Under much stress, I started nursing school. Within one year I had a recurrence of cancer. This time five doctors diagnosed me as terminal. I had surgery and radiation, and I went on with my life as if I was going to make it. I graduated with my class, passed my boards, and accepted a job as a psych nurse in a hospital where I knew no one. It was tough moving away from friends and family. During this time of treatment and change, I prayed a lot and practiced guided imagery, imagining that Pac-Men were gobbling up any cancer cells in their paths.

One night, in my new house, as I was falling asleep, I felt a presence in the room. I saw a spirit in a flowing robe and sandals. A blinding white light emanated from his hands. The light washed over me from head to toe. In that instant, I knew I was healed.

To the amazement of my doctors, and with the grace of God, I survived. I worked as a nurse in my chosen field and even practiced therapeutic touch, a contemporary healing modality drawn from ancient practices and developed by Dora Kunz and Dolores Krieger. After many of the staff and patients received my treatment, they reported relief from their ailments. I knew, then, I was just a conduit using the power I had been given.

God's Timing

BY TERESA AND TONY MAROTTA

Six years ago my husband was dying; the only solution was a liver transplant. After all the testing was done, he finally made it to the transplant list and was cleared for possible transplant if a liver was available.

Tony was only fifty years old. It was the worst time of my life as I watched him die a bit more each day and could not cure him. I could only hope that he would stay alive long enough to receive a transplant.

I woke up on Tuesday, and Tony told me about this strange event. God had talked to him. He told me, "God said I'm going to get a liver tomorrow on Friday. I almost told God tomorrow is Tuesday, but I thought I shouldn't correct God." He wanted to know what I thought this meant. I told him, "Well, I think it means you will get a liver transplant...though it could be tomorrow or it could be Friday. God's time is different than ours, but I believe you will get one sometime in the future."

Tuesday came and went and nothing happened. Friday came, and we had to go for more tests at another hospital. We looked like gunfighters at the OK Corral. I had my cell phone on; Tony had his on and his beeper. We wanted to go up to the unit and ask if they were looking for us because God's message said Friday. But nothing happened. Later, Tony told me he thought God had forgotten.

Then, at about 3:30 on Saturday afternoon, the phone call came. They had a match. By 6 PM we were there, by midnight he was on the OR table, and on July 13 he got his transplant. While at the hospital we found out that our eighteen-year-old donor had died in a car accident on Friday, and of course the tomorrow of Friday is Saturday, the day Tony got his liver. The miracle was complete.

Tony had no complications or rejection episodes, and by October he was back to work full-time and is wonderfully healthy now.

Surrender to Survive

BY SUE MEMHARD

I was a two-time breast cancer survivor. Each time, a rather unusual physician named Dr. Bernie Siegel became center stage in my world. I listened to his tapes before, during, and after surgeries, and his words held me through chemo. He believed in miracles — and so did I. Due to serious side effects, I stopped chemo prematurely, refused radiation, and yet survived — for fourteen years.

To work with the healer I thought could help save my life, my husband and I abruptly left our long-time home and our friends and family in Massachusetts, knowing we would not return. When I arrived in Denver last June, I wondered if I would see the month's end. I came on faith — faith in the energy and spiritual cancer treatment I had chosen, faith in God and a conviction that now was simply not my time to leave. I was having an advanced, aggressive metastatic breast cancer recurrence. And I felt that somehow I would survive it.

"It's never too late," my healer had pronounced. I believed her. And so the journey began.

The chemo years before had created its own legacy of health problems, and I had developed severe chemical intolerances little understood by the medical profession. In recent years I largely avoided traditional medical care. Now, unable to undergo surgical anesthesia or chemo, I had no choice but to find a completely alternative way. Bernie's enlightened teachings laid the foundation and gave me the courage to do so.

An energy and spiritual healer in Denver was the practitioner I trusted…a worker of miracles.

On my first day of "treatment," I was directed *to walk around the Denver Statehouse three times clockwise*. This of course seemed ridiculous, and I was in significant pain from the then-advanced cancer. "You can do it," we were cheerfully told. "You'll understand later."

So I did, limping, sweating, hanging onto Jim's arm, and together we rejoiced in a feeble "I can." Great, I thought, but how is this going to save me?

And then the first miracle happened: I was given time to find out.

Over the next weeks and months, my healer delivered powerful healing energy to my body in daily treatments. Together we uncovered lifetimes (yes, lifetimes) of trauma, negative beliefs, and emotions.

These were some of my (unconscious) beliefs:

It's too hard.
I can't.
I don't deserve to heal.
Maybe God doesn't love me.
My default emotional states all evolved from fear.
"This is a big project," my healer pronounced.

When not in treatments, I made prescribed dietary changes, consumed endless amounts of wheatgrass and Essiac, took handfuls of supplements, received Chinese acupuncture, and most important, was taught kundalini yoga. As the yoga practice deepened, what I had been promised came true: it was sustenance to the body and soul, life-giving as air itself.

Yet, like a bad recurring dream, "I can't" still whispered from the wings.

There was that question of God. Where was (s)he? Why had this happened to me again? Did God love me — or just everyone else, more deserving than I? I had some big repairs to make in my thinking. Despite a lifetime of spiritual seeking, despite my "belief" in miracles, the surprising truth was I had lost my faith as a child.

"God was there," I was reminded. "It was you who left."

I realized I had begun to surrender to partnership with God from the time I'd agreed to circle the Denver Statehouse three times when we first arrived. We tackled fear and its related negative emotions. How can fear coexist with God inside? I began to be aware of its pervasiveness in my life. Was there another way to be in the world? While these defensive, vigilant ways of relating to life were effective for childhood survival, they served no purpose now. In fact, *they fed the cancer.* When I was actually able to shift myself into happier internal places — love, enthusiasm, compassion, detachment, peacefulness, tolerance, patience, surrender — in spite of how my body felt, daily life, and my body, were better.

"Focus always on the light and you will heal. The body will follow the mind."

As I plowed through mental, emotional, and spiritual layers, my once-battered heart began to open. I felt light breathed into me and pain receding. The cancer tightness in my chest released.

I sent gratitude to every cell. Gratitude for miracles. Gratitude for my amazing, loving husband and daughter, and for their unquestioning support of my chosen unconventional healing path. Gratitude for this precious life.

But fear still lurked, and anger ran deeper than I thought. I needed to claim my innate empowerment, release an unconscious victim program. Finally, I understood at the deepest levels that childhood abuse and neglect necessitate forgiveness, acceptance, and letting go. Then nothing — including cancer — can have power over us.

Repeatedly I returned to surrender. The opposite of giving up, surrender to God's light and grace is fundamental to the soul's healing. Our precious little will and ego must bow to the Infinite! It seems so simple, so obvious, and yet so unattainable.

And then, one day, it isn't.

My will is thy will.

The release in my body is real. The cancer cells are dying.

Just over one year from the day we landed in Denver, I am looking out the window of our little rented house, marveling at the majestic front range, and contemplating all that has happened.

I have learned that cancer is a bully from our past. Like all dis-ease, it begins in the mind, emotions, and spirit, and appears later, often many years later, in the body. Yes, we can treat it with surgery, drugs, and other interventions to prolong life, but the soul longs for more.

For women, Mother Earth's increasing distress is a deep wounding to our divine feminine nature, whether we are aware of it or not. Our breasts, symbols of motherhood and comfort, are in pain. I understand now that allowing my own or the world's hurt to enter my body serves no one.

There are many gifts. This astonishing soul work has strengthened my faith in miracles and has created deep cellular healing. I am physically stronger and healthier than I've been in years, more conscious, loving, tolerant, peaceful…happy. Another miracle: The chemical sensitivities are nearly nonexistent.

For the first time in my life I feel whole. It took three times to get here, and I am a slow learner, but I'm healing. If it is meant to be, I will be completely well.

The truth is that my story can be anyone's. When the soul is determined to heal, the body can follow, and what we call miracles can happen. As Bernie first taught me, our true nature is wholeness, love, and happiness — and is available to us all.

Miracle Memo

Survivors have certain personality characteristics, which include a sense of humor. I know, and studies reveal, that cancer patients who laugh live longer. Just laugh and you will feel the difference in your body.

The desire to survive contributed to Bob Ellal's remarkable self-induced or miraculous healing. But it was not only his desire to see his children grow up — it was the work he did to make it happen. He became, not a good patient, but a responsible participant. He showed up for practice and learned from his coaches to put in the time and the effort and energy, and he made a difference. He changed his life, and his body got the message.

Natalie Palmer is a survivor and an example that we can learn from, whether we are facing problems or a life-threatening disease. While Natalie had a great sense of humor, she also got mad at God. I know people who didn't start to get well until they got mad as hell at God and told God he was to cure them or let them die. Appropriate anger can mobilize our passion and energy and help the miracle of healing to occur.

The universe is filled with energy, and I do believe, as Marilyn Gilliom does, that we are all conduits for this energy. More studies of energy cures will be done when science and research are willing to open their minds to explore and study these methods of healing.

We are all capable of experiencing what Marilyn did and letting this energy come through us, but to do this we must be in a place of peace and faith, so internal conflict and disbelief do not hinder what it is possible for us to achieve. Miracles are a part of the nature of life. Magic happens when we live in our hearts and not in our heads, and not in the stressful world we have created through our thoughts and beliefs.

When we leave our bodies, there is no time. Energy does not experience time; matter does. So God may have confused Tony Marotta by describing when Friday would be, since for God there is only "tonow," not today and tomorrow. So live in the tonow because yesterday is gone, tomorrow is out of sight, and miracles happen tonow when God is with us.

Once again we have a treasure trove of learned wisdom, which Sue Memhard learned and shared from her experience. Sue speaks of energy healing. I have been healed by the laying on of hands; I know of healers who have healed people and animals of cancer through the use of energy healing. Energy healing is the medicine of the future.

Survivors fight for their authentic lives and not for the roles they play in them. I've known women who wanted to live because they were "mothers" and died when the kids left home. Do not live a role. If you introduce yourself to God by saying, "I am a single mom," God says, "Come back when you know who you are." You need to know you are an authentic human being made of the divine stuff and a child of God.

When you achieve that state, the voice will speak

to you and guide you. I hear inner voices, and when I do I follow their advice and the directions they give me. The result has been very gratifying and healing. We are all capable of hearing the voice if we calm our minds and listen, or use repetitive exercise, meditation, or yoga to help us be receptive.

I believe God communicates with us. My concept of God is intelligent, conscious, loving energy. Why those words? Because creation, as astronomers and quantum physicists will tell you, couldn't have been an accident. If we just move our planet a few miles, we would not survive due to temperature changes.

Miracles are our potential, and I hope minds open to this and we explore the reality of these events so they can become a part of our lives, as all miracles should be. Remember to believe in your own potential and experience, and do not close your mind to what you cannot explain.

Become a good one: a divine,
authentic creation that you design and create,
and not a role imposed upon you by others.

CHAPTER FIVE

Redirections

Sometimes we look for those thunderous things to happen in our life for our lives to change or go in the other direction. We seek the miracle. We seek the parting of the seas, the moving of the mountains. But no, it's a quiet thing. At least for me it was.

— *Ben Vereen*

When the worst event becomes the *best* event, it is what I call a spiritual flat tire. When you get a flat and are very upset about being late, and then learn your life was saved by being late to the airport and missing a plane that crashed, you bless the flat tire. I always see a problem as a gift, wake-up call, or new beginning.

My mother used to drive me nuts whenever I had a problem, saying, "It was meant to be. God is redirecting you. Something good will come of this." What she taught me was that I didn't know the future, to keep an open mind and see what God had in store for me.

You must be able to love and accept yourself and life's difficulties and not see them as God punishing you. God is not the problem but a resource and a loving Creator.

A friend I knew went to commit suicide by jumping in front of a subway train, and the train was delayed. His life was saved, and this event helped him to redirect his life and find love. Who worked that one out?

We are never alone. I know we have collective consciousness and spirit guides with us at all times. The problem is that our minds are rarely quiet enough to be aware of them. If we are in turmoil, the pond, which reflects our life and essence, is never still enough for us to be in touch with this wisdom and meaning. We need to pay attention to the so-called detours; they may be miracles in the making.

You can find five of my favorite stories of redirections in this chapter. Dede Norungolo shares how a tragic, life-changing car accident became her life's biggest blessing; Cynthia Husted writes about a black widow spider bite that led her to become the textile artist she is today; Cathy Scibelli decided not to listen to her doctor's death sentence, but to follow her heart, mind, and body instead and activate her survivor personality; Marie DeHaan tells how she stood up for her treatment choices despite pressure from a forceful nurse; and Michelle Civalier shares how a friend changed her goals when a debilitating disease left her unable to meet her original dreams.

The Worst/Best Thing
I Can't Remember, but Won't Forget

BY DEDE NORUNGOLO

On June 10, 1999, I made a decision that I would, one, not ever remember and, two, never forget. It was on that day, the one-year anniversary of the death of a friend's father, that I set out in my trusty all-wheel-drive SUV toward her residence near Buladean, North Carolina. I traveled along a two-lane highway to arrive at my friend's property. Although I arrived unannounced, she assured me I was welcome.

After a few days, I waved good-bye and that was all I could remember. From my friend's account, and the tales of a volunteer rescue squad member, I was driving away from her place that summer afternoon on Highway 226 in a rainstorm and my vehicle hydroplaned, sending me off an embankment to rest in a creek near a farmhouse. I would later read the police report and see the officer's notation of "driving too fast for conditions." I suffered a mild traumatic brain injury on that day.

The miracle began the moment someone heard metal on rock and called 911. Then, members of the Fork Mountain Rescue Squad converged, and I would learn, years later, from one responder over a lunch designed to thank him that the day of my wreck was the first time he'd used the Jaws of Life.

Apparently, the rescue squad had only recently

completed a successful fundraiser, prior to the June 1999 wreck, to buy the equipment he had to rely on to pull me from my vehicle. And not only was the volunteer a member of the rescue squad, but he also was my friend's plumber — the friend I'd gone to visit that fateful day.

Because of Jack Goodwin and the other volunteers, I was transported to the Level I Trauma Center, where members of the Wings crew would later meet with my friend and family members.

Today, I feel blessed — yes, blessed that the worst/best thing that ever happened to me has propelled me into a career as a certified rehabilitation counselor, able to work with other traumatic brain injury survivors and individuals with disabilities.

I liken this to a God wink or certainly a "gentle" nudge in the right direction. I can trace my journey from the time of the wreck to this day, by connecting the individuals together who have encouraged me, redirected me, and loved me through each day.

I've connected with spirit guides, been approached by a shaman with a message for me, and realized we are never alone. Once fear abates, there really is nothing but love and healing. This miracle — my miracle — is living a life of service and advocacy for others now.

Tradition, Interrupted

BY MICHELLE CIVALIER

My friend Melissa has forgotten my birthday for sixteen years. Although time has put various forms of distance between us, her yearly lapse in memory is the tradition that reminds me to keep in touch with old friends. My birthday would pass to the tune of crickets singing, I would hassle her about it through email, and she would respond with faux declarations of repentance and excuses, as well as an update on her life. So when she missed my twenty-ninth birthday, I happily sent my typical woeful message, anxious to hear how life was treating her.

I was a bit surprised when she didn't reply. While forgetting my birthday was expected, the failure to acknowledge it after the fact was a new twist. Four months later, I received my apology in a poorly typed, short email that made me instantly sick to my stomach.

Melissa explained she had missed my birthday because she had been in the hospital. She was quite sorry, but she was just regaining movement of two of her fingers, and typing was exhausting. The letters "GBS GBS GBS" were written in place of her signature, like a frantic, silent scream.

Guillain-Barre syndrome, or GBS, is a rare, poorly understood autoimmune disorder in which the body attacks itself, specifically the peripheral nervous system. Doctors attempted to stop her creeping paralysis with intravenous immunoglobulin, a standard treatment to slow the progression of GBS and lessen the severity of symptoms. Unfortunately for Melissa, it had the reverse effect. As time slowed down to accommodate her thoughts, she went from panicked to calmly accepting of that which she could not control — the fragility of life.

But death was not her destiny yet. Gradually, she regained the ability to tap her fingers on the sheet, then twitch her wrists a bit to the side, and flex her feet. Each day brought a new little milestone that was met with cheers and encouragement from loved ones. Her prognosis shifted from "unlikely" to "most definitely."

Her relationship with her fiancé teetered between being a stabilizing force and her biggest worry. After all, he was forced to shoulder the responsibility of not only running the household but also managing Melissa's various disabilities, ranging from cooking her food to pushing her wheelchair, all the while working a full-time job. In the end, the only exasperation he expressed was in response to her feelings of guilt: "Melissa! Love is not a burden!" His total acceptance of her new body made her determined to heal, as much for him as for herself.

Although physically she was making incredible strides, Melissa was having difficulty reconciling to the unexpected direction life had taken her. "What if I never accomplish my goals?" she sobbed to her mother, a hardworking perfectionist who had made sacrifices in her own life to ensure her daughter would be better than the best.

"So what?" Melissa's mother apparently didn't care. "Set different goals."

And so she did. After six months of grueling physical therapy, Melissa walked down the aisle at her wedding. Shortly after that, she returned to her career as a counselor for troubled youth. She enlisted the help of a professional to assist her with some lingering post-traumatic stress, but otherwise, she has released the paralyzing grip GBS had on both her body and her mind.

Today, Melissa is living a normal life off of her medications. I'm not sure if her recovery is due to strength of mind, strength of body, or the strength of something else. Regardless, she lost to chance, and then promptly beat the odds, living to tell a miraculous story.

Of course, while her recovery is impressive, the real miracle is that I received an ecard from Melissa's work email on my thirtieth birthday, perfectly typed with all her fingers.

Black Widow Spider

BY CYNTHIA HUSTED

I learned the miracle of transformation from a black widow spider. Working in a garden one afternoon, I was bitten by a black widow spider. I had a rare auto-immune response to the venom and nearly died, spent six months in bed with a spastic paralysis, and lost my short- and long-term memory. To this day, I have a partial paralysis and small fiber neuropathy over my entire body.

When hospitalized, I found myself deliberately twisting the fingers of my two hands together and could not stop. I was curious and did not know what I was doing. It was not until years later when I began knitting, because my fingers would not move, that I realized I was going through the knitting motions while in the hospital. It was as if my higher self was telling me that this would be my therapy. I had to learn to use my brain and body again, and knitting was a way to get my fingers moving and to help restore cognitive functions.

After making thirty simple scarves, I put the knitting aside because I was having trouble learning something new and did not want to admit it. I kept pushing, determined to get back into my old world of logic and intellect and life as a scientist. A few years later when I continued to have difficulties with cognitive functions, an occupational therapist encouraged me to learn something new, and so I took a knitting class and have not stopped since.

While I'm still recovering, the patterns in my knitting emerge from a deep place of resonance. The exquisite fibers of mohair, cashmere, silk, and alpaca in my knitting help to stimulate my C fibers, small sensory nerves that were damaged through my entire body. The spider medicine infuses into my designs and assists with my recovery. I honor the spider with this creative journey.

His Holiness the Dalai Lama has said that a miracle is when the unexpected occurs, something we cannot understand. For me, the unexpected was the healing power of art. I deliberately sought to do all the intellectually right things to balance my physical, emotional, and spiritual selves, but it was ultimately creative expression that allowed healing and transformation to occur. Contained within every stitch is a prayer or mantra, and I send these blessings to you.

God Is Redirecting You

BY CATHY SCIBELLI

In the middle of a biopsy on my right breast, the doctor said in a scornful tone, "I'm not going to get your hopes up. This is cancer. And you have a 'mass' under your arm, too. This is what happens when you don't get a yearly mammogram." He suggested that I might not want to share this news with my family just yet, until I could "break it to them gently." He then proceeded to go into a hallway and make a phone call to an oncologist friend, telling him loud enough for me to hear, "I have a stage-four cancer patient I'm going to send you."

On May 27, 2010, my oncologist said to me, "You have healed so well, I hold you up as an example to all my patients. I tell them how you took a horrible situation and turned it into something positive, accomplishing new goals and truly enjoying life instead of letting fear dominate you. You could be the poster child for our center. Go home and enjoy your summer, and I'll see you for your next checkup in September."

What happened in the eighteen months between those two doctor visits?

I came home from that first doctor visit feeling terrified and doomed. I searched on the Internet for some thread of hope to hold on to, and I found Dr. Bernie Siegel. I bought his book *Love, Medicine*

& Miracles and some of his CDs. He told me that I didn't have to give up, and that "something good will come from this. God is redirecting you."

I decided to take his advice to "fire" the doctor who had been so cold. I reached out to family and friends for support and asked everyone I knew if they could recommend a breast surgeon. When three people who didn't know each other gave me the same name — Dr. K — I called that doctor. Dr. K turned out to be not just a skilled surgeon but a wonderful human being as well. She directed me to an oncologist who put me at ease the first time I met her. Both doctors hugged me, they never mentioned stages of cancer, and when they used statistics, it was to impress upon me that people can survive cancer. I went for a battery of tests, and it turned out the cancer had not spread outside the breast/lymph nodes.

I then underwent several months of chemotherapy with almost no side effects, which amazed my oncologist. I told her about Dr. Siegel and how I was imagining that the chemo drugs were powerful medicine that would heal me. I think she thought I was a little crazy at this point, but she said, "Well, whatever you're doing, keep doing it, because it's working." The tumor shrunk tremendously, and my immune system stayed strong.

I began to look at doctors in a new way after reading Dr. Siegel's advice about forming a partnership with your doctor and becoming an individual to them. My surgeon keeps the cards I send her in my file and laughs about them when I see her. I meet my radiologist in Whole Foods, and we hug and chat like old friends. I share my personal triumphs and family stories with my oncologist. I never would have imagined that doctors would be some of my best friends, true partners in a healing journey.

I had always wanted to be a writer, but never had the courage to actually try it seriously. When I read stories in Dr. Siegel's books about people who had completely changed their careers after having cancer, I started writing. I feel as if I'm finally doing something I love and something that gives me a chance to be that beacon of "love, joy, hope, and optimism" for others.

But the change I enjoy most is that I learned to say no to people and stop being the "good girl." That in itself is a miracle!

When I look back to that first diagnosis eighteen months ago, I truly feel as if I have experienced a miracle in my life, not just in surviving the cancer, but in learning to thrive in a new life that is so rich and rewarding. I really believe that Dr. Siegel is an angel living among us.

Let Me Be Exceptional

BY MARIE DeHAAN

It was quiet in the chemo ward… until the clinical trial nurse showed up.

"So, Marie, how is your radiation going?"

I instantly felt the hackles rise on the back of my neck. This nurse knew I wasn't doing radiation, and I resented her pretending to engage me in a pleasant conversation. We were talking about matters of life and death here — literally — and I was sick of thinking about this decision.

"Oh, I've elected not to do radiation, Sharon," I said, as sweet as pie. Two could play at this game.

"What? Radiation is standard treatment. You will be yanked off the clinical trial for being noncompliant."

"Sharon," I continued, calm and syrupy, "we both know that this trial is testing the difference between patients having lapatinib and Herceptin versus those having one or the other alone." Did she think she could pull one over on me?

I may have stage-three, locally advanced breast cancer, but I'm not stupid.

"It's standard treatment," she repeated.

Why didn't she just call me an idiot to my face in front of all the other nurses and sick patients while she was at it?

"Oh, Sharon, guess what? I got my new prosthesis from Nordstrom." I did an about-face. "Yep. Went from a size double D to a size G. Can you believe it?"

She stared at me. I threw her off guard. I think she wanted me to wilt under her gaze, and I wasn't going to budge.

"Marie," she began again, her voice getting louder with each sentence, "you were supposed to start that radiation several weeks ago. It's probably too late to start it now."

I felt a small niggle of uncertainty. What if she was right? What if my decision was the wrong one and ended with a coffin and my family and friends gathered around wailing, "If she had only done that radiation..."?

It's not like we were picking out shoes here. Or even a different size boob to replace the one that I had recently had cut from my body.

In my previous life, I would have mumbled "okay" and plodded along like a sheep to the slaughter when the doctor advised that I needed radiation. At the minimum, I would have started bawling like a baby when Sharon gave me heck for not getting my act together and signing up for the nearest radiation center.

Somehow, cancer was making me assertive in ways I never thought possible.

"Sharon, the surgeon said doing radiation would only add 3 percent to the odds that this breast cancer will not kill me. That number is not big enough for me."

"What does he know?"

Okay, this nurse was really ticking me off now.

"Oh, he's only been a doctor for thirty-two years, specializing in breast cancer, and he didn't give me a hard time like you are."

I didn't say this to her, of course. Instead, I said, "Did I tell you about the nice lady at Nordstrom? Her name was Alyssa, and she was really nice." Maybe you could take some lessons from her, I wanted to add.

Her face flushed red with anger. "Standard treatment."

By this time, I wanted to stand up on my chair and yell, "I'm an exceptional patient! Bernie Siegel would be proud and applaud my admirable bravery! I have my own brain, and I don't have to do what you say!"

The only problem was, I was strapped to my Herceptin IV bag and couldn't move. Besides, there were sick people all around us, and I refused to stoop to her level.

"Sharon," I said, firmly, "if I made the wrong decision here, *I* will be the one to ultimately pay for this decision with my life. It will affect you in no way, whatsoever."

That was over three months ago.

When I returned home from that appointment, I contacted Sharon's supervisor and quietly, calmly, and reasonably pulled out of the clinical trial. I was going to protect myself at all costs.

My last follow-up test showed that I am cancer-free. More than that, I learned to stand up for myself and my hard-earned size-G prosthesis. We both have some exceptional living left to do.

Miracle Memo

When I lecture, I hold up a piece of paper with a black dot on it and ask people, "What am I holding in my hand?" Those who only see the worst in life say, "A black dot." Then I point out to them that I am holding a piece of white paper with a black dot and that it represents everyone's life.

We are all wounded, but some of us, like Dede Norungolo, turn the darkness into light and the charcoal into a diamond. Dede had a spiritual flat tire that led her to a place of deep gratitude. The training of Dede's rescuers and their available equipment speaks to the fact that there are no coincidences.

Michelle Civalier wrote of her friend, Melissa, whose fiancé's words had me close to tears: "Love is not a burden." He is a special man. When I think of how rare it is for men to show up at support group meetings or accompany their loved ones to the doctor, I am touched by what a special guy he is. Melissa has her miracle right there.

Goals are not the issue, either. Melissa's mother is right. When life closes one door, further down the corridor another one will be open; just change your goals. Look what Helen Keller taught the world despite her afflictions. Your goal can be becoming strong at the broken places and flying despite a broken wing. As Thornton Wilder wrote, "In love's service only the wounded soldiers can serve."

My wife has lived with multiple sclerosis for many

decades, and it has taken its toll. Now I am the caregiver, and during one of my frustrating moments, she said the same thing to me: "I love you. You love me. Everything is all right." Yes, she is still teaching me to stop being the doctor and be her compassionate lover. Then we both feel so good.

I am an artist and portrait painter, and I realized how healing art can be after I injured my back and could not stand up unless I was painting or operating upon someone. Then I could stand for hours, but when I was done, I had to lie down, as I was now back in my body and not creating.

When you create, as Cynthia Husted learned to do with her knitting, you enter a trance state and are free of bodily afflictions, and you lose awareness of time. One more thing Cynthia demonstrates is that healing and curing are two different entities. I know people who cannot be cured but are truly healed beings who are teachers for all of us, and I know others who are cured but still remain bitter, resentful, and far from being healed in their lives or bodies.

There is an artist in all of us, and when the artist is alive you become a creative, inspiring human being. I recommend the book *The Art Spirit* by Robert Henri and Margery Ryerson. Henri was a famous artist, and in his classes he combined creativity with life. He told his students to listen and not take notes. Well, Margery, who became a friend of mine years ago, said she took notes, and when she was home sick for several weeks, she put them into book form. Henri liked what she did, and together they wrote the book. I loved it and have a painting by Margery in our home. When you are an artist, the world also becomes more interesting and beautiful.

I like that Cathy Scibelli's oncologist saw her as an example of an exceptional patient. That means he was learning from her behavior that patients can get well, even when they are not supposed to, according to their doctors' thinking. The ability to have miraculous events occur is built into all living things, or we would not have survived all the various diseases and disasters of the past. Our genes are designed for survival.

Cathy also visualized her treatments as beneficial, and so her body did not have all the side effects people have. I have my "crazy" patients who have no side effects of radiation and chemo because they "get out of the way and let it go to my tumor" or see it as yellow energy flowing only to their disease. I also know of people who did not receive radiation or chemo, but thought they were and had all the side effects. The mind is a powerful resource when used properly.

In the story, Cathy referred to me as an angel. I often joke that I am an angel and on the Board of Directors of Heaven, so I do have resources that help me to help others. Some people lovingly call me Saint Bernard. Humor is a wonderful thing and very necessary.

I have a poem entitled "I Grew Up in Texas" by Cassandra Tucker. In it the woman says she was prepared for cancer because she grew up in Texas with its droughts, hurricanes, floods, and more, so she "knew how to ride things out." We all need to learn how and believe we can.

Marie DeHaan's behavior illustrates many aspects of what I call survival behavior. The first is to see that our treatment choices must be seen as the labor pains of self-birth. The pains, like radiation, chemotherapy, and surgery, are not to be imposed and prescribed by others, but accepted as our choice. Then when you give birth to yourself, they are worthwhile, just as the pain when birthing your child is worthwhile.

Also, if you choose the treatment, you have far fewer side effects than when you do it to please others. It also must be seen as a choice of what is right for you. I think it is a lot wiser to follow your heart and intuition and do what is right for you.

When you do what is right for you, you will never be angry with yourself or your decision. No matter what the future holds. One of survival behavior's important characteristics is expressing anger appropriately in defense of yourself. When you are not respected, speak up and share your feelings and anger. It may save your life some day.

The miracle here is Marie's ability "to stand up for herself" and to love and value herself and her decisions about *her* life. The majority of the world grows up with the burden of guilt, shame, and blame and, therefore, is afraid to make choices and decisions and feel empowered because they could do it wrong and would again be a failure.

When you rebirth yourself and are living the life you have chosen, rather than the one imposed by others, your body gets the message and does all it can to keep you alive. The key is always keeping your power and doing what feels right for you.

Most important for survival is this statement:
"But the change I enjoy most is that I learned
to say 'no' to people and stop being the 'good girl.'
That in itself is a miracle!"

CHAPTER SIX

Angels and Guides

Angels come to help and guide us in as many guises as there are people who need their assistance. Sometimes we see their ethereal, heavenly shadow, bright with light and radiance. Sometimes we only feel their nearness or hear their whisper. And sometimes they look no different from ourselves.

— *Eileen Elias Freeman*

O ne evening I arranged my notes on the podium and began my lecture. I noticed that what I was saying was not following my outline. I kept struggling to get back to my outline for the talk, but after a few minutes I realized the talk I had not planned was better than the one I had. So I just let the words flow out of me for the next two hours. At the conclusion of my presentation, a woman walked up to me and said, "I've heard you before. That was better than usual." The next woman came up and said, "Standing in front of you for the entire talk was this man. I drew his picture for you." When I looked at the picture I knew who it was: George.

George is my inner guide, whom I met when

doing guided imagery, as a nonbeliever, for the first time. The picture she drew was the same as one I had drawn for Elisabeth Kübler-Ross years before. From that day forward, George does all my talks for me. They come from a place of consciousness shared with the audience.

A few years later, after delivering a funeral sermon for a friend one Sunday morning, I was standing alone in the hallway when Olga Worrall, a well-known healer, who had attended the funeral of our mutual friend, came up to me. "Bernie, are you Jewish?" I asked her if she wanted to know because I had delivered a Sunday sermon. She said, "No, it's because there are two rabbis standing next to you." Her description of them from their garments to their beards was again exactly like George. I think his presence in my life explains many of my miraculous experiences.

I have been in four life-threatening accidents, including choking nearly to death, car collisions, and falling off the roof when a ladder broke. Each time I walked away with no serious injuries. I said to an audience one night, "I must have an angel."

I believe we all have angels or guides. I can't help but think of the story of the lady who hears a voice say, "Jump back." She does and realizes she would have been hit by a bus if she kept crossing the street. It's a good thing she listened!

We must remember that there is always hope. We are capable of amazing things, and when we do not fear failure, we have nothing to lose by attempting to achieve the miraculous.

Angels Have Charge over Me

BY SYLVIA BRIGHT-GREEN

To retire up north in the woods on a lake was something my husband and I dreamt about for years. So when we heard of a resort going condo with its cottages in October of 1995, we seized the opportunity to rent one with an option to buy. One week later, after we moved to Lake George in Rhinelander, Wisconsin, two hundred miles from family and friends, my husband died of a heart attack.

The evening following my husband's funeral, sitting among dozens of unpacked boxes, I felt reality set in. After forty years of having someone to talk to, to hold me, and to say goodnight to, I was alone. I was totally alone.

Fear, insecurity, anger, pain, and thoughts questioning my reason for existing gripped my being. How would I survive the loneliness? Worse yet, having a deep fear of the dark since I was eight years old, I wondered, how would I get through the nights? The thought of not being able to sleep in safety anymore had me running through the house locking all the doors and windows. I even braced the doors under the knobs with chairs. I closed all the curtains and turned on all the lights. I placed a flashlight next to my bed (in case the electricity went out, I told myself) and my husband's hunting knife under my pillow.

Still, I couldn't sleep. In addition to my sleep

malady and my loneliness and insecurity, I was the only resident in this resort during one of the most debilitating snowstorms to hit Oneida County in over fifty years. These grief symptoms kept me confined and on my pity-pot for three months.

Then one January evening everything changed. I was sitting in my living room recliner watching television, eating a TV dinner, and thinking about how I didn't have much of a life anymore, when I inhaled a kernel of corn. Coughing and choking, I jumped up from the recliner and proceeded to pound my back into a protruding doorframe, in hopes of forcing the corn from my windpipe. That didn't work. To make matters worse, during the coughing and choking siege, my bladder let loose, and I had to run for the bathroom.

While sitting on the commode, I continued to cough and choke for what seemed like forever. Yet even with all the coughing, I still couldn't dislodge the kernel of corn from my windpipe. I started panicking when a light-headed feeling along with clamminess started creeping throughout my body. Was this how I was supposed to die, choking on a kernel of corn? I knew I'd been depressed with doubts and fears about how I was going to go on or even survive without my husband. But the actual possibility of dying alone and not being found for days had me silently praying.

"Oh, God," I inwardly said, as tears washed down my cheeks. "I don't really want to die. I do have a life, and I value it. So if you can help me, please do it now."

No sooner had the words exited my mind than

suddenly I felt a forceful blow hit me between my shoulder blades, sending the corn flying from my windpipe, out of my mouth, and into the shower stall. Startled, I half-turned and looked behind me as if someone could be there, though this was impossible, since my back was up against the commode, which was up against the wall. Yet I definitely felt a hard blow to my upper back, almost knocking me off the commode. But, I wondered, who could have done it?

Just then I remembered a Bible verse my older sister, Peggy, used to say to me as a child to calm my fears: "For it is written, he shall give his angels charge over thee, to keep thee in all his ways."

"Thank you, God, for sending one of your angels to keep me safe."

Later, as I was preparing for bed, it occurred to me that I didn't have to be afraid of the dark and being alone anymore. After all, if an angel isn't going to let me die over a kernel of corn, I reasoned, then it is not going to allow anything to happen to me. I had now conquered my fear of the dark and being alone, all because God had sent an angel to have charge over me.

Send Me an Angel

BY SISTER PATRICIA DOTZAUER

I am a Catholic sister residing in New Jersey. In November 1995 I was diagnosed with a malignant lump in my breast. The first surgeon told me I had a choice to have either a lumpectomy or mastectomy. It was up to me. The lump was stage two because of its size — five centimeters. He had absolutely no opinion either way. He was not helping me with a decision I didn't know how to make.

I went to pray about it, and the story of the Agony in the Garden came to me. I opened the Bible and read it over and over. I kept saying to God, "Send me an angel to tell me what to do." A sister in my community, who is also a medical doctor, arranged for me to have a second opinion with a breast surgeon located in New Jersey. My appointment was five days away. For five days I prayed the same prayer, "Send me an angel to tell me what to do."

As I awaited the doctor in the examining room, I was not aware of the office policy for her staff. No one, nurses or herself, wore white coats. They all wore regular clothing. She had all my previous testing results. She walked into the room, introduced herself, put my mammogram film up on the screen, and turned around. That's when I saw it. On the lapel of her jacket was an angel pin, and she looked at me and said, "Sister, you have to have a mastectomy. You have no other choice; your tumor is too large."

Later in her office, as I looked around the room filled with an image of Our Lady of Guadalupe and numerous other religious symbols, she said to me, "Have you ever heard of Saint Ignatius Loyola?" Of course I said yes. "You are about to begin a spiritual journey," she said. "You have a mountain to climb, and I will be your guide."

She continued, "Talk to me and tell me what you are feeling."

"I'm afraid," I said.

Without skipping a beat, she said, "You are not going to die."

That was fourteen and a half years ago. I truly believe God sent me the angel I prayed for in the form of my doctor.

Through the TV Waves

BY MARILYN BECKER GILLIOM

In 2004, I fell and hit the back of my head on the ice. A CT scan, MRI, and neurological evaluation showed a concussion. (Have a nice day!) Meanwhile, I had maybe fifteen TIAs, or ministrokes, which coincided with low blood sugar. My endocrinologist lowered my insulin dose. After eighty days, I was diagnosed with a subdural hematoma and had to have cranial surgery. I lost my speech and use of my right arm and leg. We weren't able to get rehab for me because we had recently changed health insurance companies.

I began working toward my recovery. As a psych nurse, I knew about the pathways in the brain. I suffered with confusion, memory loss, and depression. Neuropsychological testing showed hope for recovery.

My husband's mother died, and he had to travel for her funeral. I was all alone, mostly helpless, in pain, and very down. I kept hearing a dismal voice in my head saying, "Take it all, take all the insulin." One night, very distraught, I sat on the couch and the television came on. (I guess I sat on the remote!) A nun, Mother Angelica, on EWTN told me, "You cannot kill yourself. God loves you." As a child, I had been catechized by nuns and attended mass daily before falling away from the church. I had never heard of EWTN before. I left it on day and night watching all this programming about God. I couldn't talk, but I sang all the Latin responses that I had learned as a girl. We later learned that Mother Angelica was talking to a caller who had a gun to his head. The program was a repeat filmed four years earlier, yet it spoke to me just when I needed to hear and be reminded that God has a plan for me.

Hand of an Angel

BY CINDY HURN

Asking my sweetheart if he believed in divine intervention, I received the reply, "Oh yes," with conviction. This surprised me because Rich leans toward the skeptic when concerning matters of spiritual nature. If he were convinced of an angel's interception, then I wanted to hear the story! It took place, he said, about thirty years ago, when he and his first wife, Kathy, were driving through Oregon.

"On our first night we stayed at a little motel near the Rogue River," Rich said, "and being a warm summer evening, we sat outside the cabin. A German couple from the cabin next door also sat outside. We noticed their distinctive accents and asked where they came from, and that started a pleasant evening of conversation.

"The next morning, Kathy and I packed up and drove north through the Cascade Range, hoping to visit Crater Lake, over seven thousand feet above sea level. As we approached the north entrance to the park, we heard on the radio that the park road was closed due to snow and thick fog. We couldn't believe our ears — it was June! Disappointed, we continued south toward Fort Klamath and discovered a southern entrance to the park that was still open. The ranger at the gate didn't charge us the entrance fee because, he said, we wouldn't be able to see anything through the fog.

"As we drove up the crater mountain, the fog grew thicker and thicker, with light snow falling, making visibility extremely poor. When we reached the parking lot, we crawled to a stop in front of a short stone wall. If you held your hand out, you could hardly see it, the fog was so thick. We knew the lake was somewhere behind the wall, so I stepped up onto the wall, thinking I would at least walk down to the lake's edge. At that moment, we heard another car drive into the parking lot and stop. A distinct voice with German accent reached through the fog, so I stepped down from the wall and walked over with my wife to greet the couple we'd met the evening before. After chatting for a short while, we all felt chilled to the bone, and since the weather didn't improve, we climbed back into our cars and drove out of the park.

"The next year, my wife and I took our newborn son back to the same spot. It was a beautiful, clear summer day. We drove up the same southerly entrance route. I parked, facing the same stone wall, got out, and prepared to step onto the wall, as I had done the year before. But when I looked over, there was nothing, no foothold, no ledge, nothing except a thousand-foot drop. My knees suddenly went weak; I realized just how close I had come to dying the previous year.

"If it hadn't been for perfect timing, and for the distinct accent of our German friends, I would have stepped over that wall. My wife would be a young widow, and our son would never have been conceived. I was a split second away, virtually on the edge of death. I honestly believe that some angel — some divine hand of intervention — stepped in and pulled me back from that edge."

Serendipity or Miracle?

BY SANDY MILIEFSKY

I was speaking to my cancer counselor, and she asked me how I came to attend Dr. Bernie's support group. I explained how I heard Bernie on a show. My counselor told me she knew Bernie, and then told me this story:

Years ago she had a rare form of cancer and was in Yale–New Haven Hospital, very frightened after the surgery. She said she looked up and saw a man standing in the doorway of her room, and he was surrounded by a white light. She said the man walked up to her, came face to face, and said, "You are going to live." She said that man was Bernie Siegel. She took his words seriously, and as a survivor, went on to help other survivors through the center where she helps me now. I won't call this serendipity. Not then or now.

Miracle Memo

When you need help because you are not able to handle the difficult times of life, angels step in. They are messengers. God also speaks through us, and I believe that is where those words of reassurance come from. I have found that at times I have said things to patients that I had no intention of saying and felt the words came from, as my wife says, "God knows where."

In Sylvia Bright-Green's experience with living on her own, she found there is a big difference between being alone and being lonely. When you know yourself, you will find that being alone is not a problem, and when you have faith you will also never truly feel alone. Think about how safe Sylvia felt after the angel became a part of her life. Angels come in many forms, and you can bring them into your life, from pets to people. The angels remind us to enjoy the experience and the journey and to live in our heart where miracles happen.

"Ask and you shall receive. Knock and the door will be opened." If you do not pray, which is talking to God, why should you expect God to respond? When you need help because you are not able to handle the difficult times of life, God steps in. When you are capable of creating a new self, God steps back; you order CDs, read books, and create a new self, and you don't need to ask for an angel because now you know they are always with you. Sister Patricia Dotzauer did just that in her experience with cancer. I can't help but add a bit of humor from Lily Tomlin: "When you talk to God, it's called prayer. When God talks to you, it's called schizophrenia."

We are all satellite dishes, remote controls, and TV screens. There are many voices or channels that we are exposed to, and we are given a mind, like a remote control, which we use to choose the program we are going to tune in to, to guide us through life. Our bodies, like a TV screen, then demonstrate the program we are acting out. When we choose to listen to the love channel, then we accomplish and learn what we are all here for.

Rich and Cindy Hurn certainly experienced guardian angels. Often, we are not in the mood to listen to what they are telling us because we are thinking and not feeling our way through life. Is it a coincidence that Marilyn Gilliom sat on the remote and turned it on to the channel she needed to watch? I don't think so. It helped her to love herself and feel worthy of life. We must remember that there is always hope. We are capable of amazing things, and when we do not fear failure, we have nothing to lose by attempting to achieve the miraculous.

Sandy Miliefsky exemplifies how chance meetings can change lives — even save lives — and inspire others to do the same, like a line of dominoes paying each miracle forward.

Life is never an easy journey. The way to get there

is to have faith in yourself and look for angels to guide you over the tough terrain until you find your way.

Miracles and angels are a part of our lives,
so anticipate them and tune in
through your quiet mind.

CHAPTER SEVEN

The Gift of Love

Miracles occur naturally as expressions of love. The real miracle is the love that inspires them. In this sense everything that comes from love is a miracle.

— *Marianne Williamson*

A teenager complained that her grandmother's house did not have a full-length mirror to see how she looked. Her grandmother responded by saying, "If you want to see how beautiful you are, come here and look in my eyes."

I believe love is the answer to every question you could ever ask. It is the solution to every problem, and it is necessary for our survival. When we choose to love, we can never be wrong. We will always be in the right place at the right time because love brings order, harmony, and peace.

By the same token, being loved is the gift of a lifetime. To be accepted by someone means they are transcending all your flaws with a commitment. Love is blind to our faults and flaws. I believe that, while we choose whom we love, we are wired with the desire to love from the time of our birth.

Many people believe they have some terrible defect at the center of their being, which they must hide if they are to have any chance for love. Because they believe they are unlovable and condemned to loneliness if their true selves become known, such individuals set up defenses against sharing their innermost feelings with anyone. They fear and avoid relationships.

I cared for a teenage girl with severe burn scars who wore a turtleneck even on hot summer days because she felt she was "ugly." Weeks after I suggested she spend her summer working as an aide in a nursing home, where they wore uniforms that would reveal her scars, she found the people there didn't notice them. "This is because when you are giving love," I said, "you are beautiful."

Love is energy, so it knows no time and no physical limitations. I know from my experience — personally, and through mystics, dreams, and drawings — that we are capable of communicating with animals and the dead and can know the future. I think that when two people are constantly conscious of each other it sustains a connection, which eventually leads to their being reunited.

All we can ask of life is to be given the chance to love.

All in God's Time: Rich Eldredge's Story

BY C. J. CROKER

Every night in Vietnam I sat looking at her photo, wondering if I'd ever see her again. I'd think about that first night on the Cape, three years before, when she asked me to dance; how I held her close, and how we spent the following week chaperoned by her sister, who watched over her since their mother died. When she went home to Connecticut, we wrote every week, and I drove down to see her whenever I could. Finally my draft number came up, so I joined the air force, and in my third year, I volunteered for Vietnam. During that time, I stopped writing. A lot of guys died out there; I probably would, too.

When I finally got stateside, I called her sister in San Francisco, trying to find my girl again. But her sister didn't answer the phone. It was my sweetheart's voice on the end of that line. "I'm in Sacramento," I said. "Can I come to see you?" She said yes, so I got there as quick as I could, and we spent that night together. She said she was only visiting; that now she lived on a farm in Canada and was hitchhiking back the next day. I asked her to stay with me in Sacramento, but she was determined to get back to her animals. "Come to Canada," she said, but I couldn't without going AWOL. So I just said, "No."

The next morning, I drove my girl to the I-5 on-ramp. I asked her once again, "Stay with me." But she wouldn't, so I had to let her go. She walked onto that ramp all alone and stuck her thumb out, determined to get back home, a thousand miles north of me, and I drove off, praying she'd be okay while my heart broke apart. In time, I found someone else. I went to the auction to buy furniture for my bachelor pad and came back with a new girlfriend — the auctioneer's daughter.

Over the years I wondered about my first love. I had a recurring dream that a young girl walked into my office, saying her mother said that if she ever died, the daughter was to find me, and that I would look after her. I guess because my sweetheart's mom died so young, my dream figured she would, too. Every time I traveled to another place, I looked up her name in the phone book, but she was never in it. I even drove past her old house with my wife when we went back east for a vacation, but I knew she wouldn't be there. All I found were good memories and a sad heart that didn't belong in a marriage, so I set those thoughts aside and appreciated my life in California with a beautiful woman and two great kids.

Thirty-four years later I sat in my office in Sacramento, divorced and still wondering what happened to my first love. One of these "find your classmates" programs popped onto my screen, so I typed in her name and details. Suddenly, there it was. I paid for her email address without any guarantee that it was current. I wrote, "Hi. This is Rich from Cape Cod. Remember me?" I pressed SEND, and a wave of emotion flooded over me. I knew if she didn't answer, I'd give up looking for her. This was the last time.

That was nearly ten years ago. The day before, she was in her office in England telling her secretary about her first love, saying that she'd always thought about me, wondering if I was happy and okay. Now that her marriage had ended, and her daughter was soon getting married, she was making plans to leave after the wedding and start a new life in the States or Canada. While she navigated the Internet, the same program popped up on her screen that appeared on mine. She entered her email address, hoping to reconnect with an old girlfriend, never suspecting I was looking for her. The next day, I found her and sent that first email.

We wrote to each other every day after that. It seemed as if we'd each had to fulfill a different set of responsibilities, with predestined people to love and care for. We'd each done our best and were grateful for the lives we'd had. But now, a miraculous chance with perfect timing put us back in touch. Over the next six months our old love blossomed, and I asked her once again to come and stay with me. She promised to drop in for a visit on her way to the Pacific Northwest.

She kept her promise. Nine years later, she's still here in Sacramento and we're happily in love. She's still on her way north, but she's waiting for me to retire in three years so we can go there together. We were given a second chance to fulfill our love, and we're taking that chance because we know that it's finally our time.

Daddy and Raggedy Ann

BY TERRI ELDERS

One afternoon when Grandma visited me at my hospital bed, she said that Daddy would visit me on Sunday. I knew some things, like all the names of the days of the week, but I didn't know how many days it was until Sunday. I'd just turned five that summer of 1942, and I was so proud I could hold up a whole handful of fingers when anybody asked my age.

When Grandma first brought me there, I'd heard the doctor who poked around my chest say it would take a miracle to save me. So I wanted to ask Daddy what a miracle was. Every time I heard footsteps by the door, I prayed it would be Daddy. He was in the navy, and I longed to see him in his sailor suit.

Then one morning, just after the nurse finished pounding on my chest and had made me breathe in some horrid nose drops, Daddy appeared in his navy blue bell bottom trousers and shirt trimmed with white stripes. He carried a big brown bag.

I was so happy to see him that I tried to sit up, but as soon as I lifted my head from the pillow I broke into a chorus of coughs. Daddy hurried over and leaned down to kiss my forehead. "She feels awfully warm," he said to the nurse, placing his bag on the floor next to my bed.

"That's to be expected with pneumonia. But she's past the worst part, we think."

"Daddy, I fell down at the Piggly Wiggly," I said. "My chest hurts." I remembered shaking so hard that my teeth chattered when Grandma carried me to the car and drove me to the hospital. When the doctors said that my lips had turned blue because I had double pneumonia, she started to cry and that scared me.

Daddy sat by my bed for a long time. He said he soon would sail off to fight in the war.

When the nurse brought me some warm apple juice, Daddy encouraged me to sip some, even though I found it so hard to swallow. "If you finish your juice, I've got a surprise for you in the bag."

Even though it hurt, I downed all my juice. Then Daddy opened the bag and took out a doll with two button eyes, red yarn hair, and a cute little triangle nose. She wore a blue flowered dress.

"It's Raggedy Ann," I cried with delight. I hugged the doll close, and then remembered I had something to ask Daddy about.

"Daddy, what's a miracle?"

"It's something wonderful that happens that you don't expect. For instance, let's unbutton your doll's dress." Daddy helped me slip the buttons out of the loops. I was surprised to see the little red heart on her chest. It had some letters on it. "It says 'I love you.' I want you to remember that I love you after my ship sails out."

Weeks passed before Grandma finally took me home, but I had Raggedy Ann there to comfort me through the coughing fits, runny noses, and headaches.

When I finally got up from that hospital bed, I couldn't quite remember how to walk because I had been down so long. It took a few days before once again I grew steady on my feet.

Two years later when Daddy returned from the war, he came to Grandma's house, and I showed him how I had learned to tap dance. We danced together, humming "Grand Old Flag."

Several years later I learned that in 1942 it was still commonplace for children to die of bronchial pneumonia. I indeed had been lucky to survive. It wasn't until the close of World War II that miracle drugs appeared on the home front in the form of penicillin and other antibiotics, and countless children's lives were saved.

Decades later, I worked for the Peace Corps, providing technical assistance to health projects in dozens of developing countries. To my astonishment I learned from the World Health Organization that pneumonia is still the forgotten killer of children, causing two million deaths worldwide, more than any other disease…more than HIV/AIDS, malaria, and measles combined. I urged our child and maternal health program managers to train Peace Corps volunteers how to alert parents in developing countries to the symptoms of this deadly disease so their children could get access to needed treatment.

That my life was spared in childhood so that I could help spare the lives of other children might just be coincidence…but I think it might have been a miracle. I only regret that when I looked at Raggedy Ann's heart on her chest, I forgot to look to see if she had wings on her back. As for Daddy, well, he was never an angel, but he sure could dance like one!

Becca's Rainbow

BY FRANCINE BROTTMAN

Bernie's wisdom was a gift to me as I navigated the waters of my daughter's cancer journey. Throughout her illness and after her passing, I read Bernie's books and exchanged correspondence with him. One of my favorite quotes from Bernie is, "We must realize people are not living or dying but alive or dead. Label someone terminal and he is treated as dead. This is wrong; if you are alive, you can still participate by loving, laughing, and living." This describes my daughter so well. She lived every moment of her life fully and with the greatest love. Her life was a miracle, and I am thankful for every moment I shared with her. I would like to share the story of Becca's rainbow with you.

The doctors called us into the room of doom and gloom. Though the walls were painted in warm colors, it was cold and unforgiving in there. We sat waiting on one of the stiff couches, staring at the pictures on the wall that attempted to create feelings of serenity. A barrage of doctors and nurses piled into this crowded space to give us their bleak news.

"We're sorry," began one of the staff oncologists, breaking the awkward silence. Though we had heard this speech before, we still felt the onslaught of emotions come over us as they told us that they expected our beautiful seven-year-old daughter to soon succumb to the cancer she had so bravely fought for the past two and a half years. The timeline they gave ranged from hours to possibly a day or two.

Fortunately, Becca had a different timeline and a different plan. Over the course of her illness, we learned many valuable lessons from our young, wise daughter. She treasured every moment of her time spent on this earth. She always found a way to live in the moment and appreciate whatever glimmers of childhood she could find. Even while she was sick, she loved to play games and express herself through art and writing. Her dolls and plush animals were her friends and patients, as she practiced the procedures on them to which she had been subjected. Tea parties and wheelchair races with the nurses helped her through the monotonous days in the hospital during the early days of her illness. Between her moments of childlike innocence, Becca espoused the wisdom of a very mature soul.

The day after our talk with the doctors, to everybody's astonishment, Becca appeared to be doing better. We all looked upon this with cautious optimism. When the art therapist entered her room, Becca wanted to spend some time with her. My husband and I took this opportunity to take a brief, but much needed respite. We returned to Becca's room, trying to hide our sullen feelings in hope of providing our daughter with love and comfort. What we saw when we entered the room stunned us. Becca was happily sitting up in her bed, sculpting a rainbow out of aluminum foil and colorful tape. According to the doctors, she should have been lying in bed, dying. But here she was, proudly making the most beautiful rainbow I have ever seen. She chose hope.

Still, we knew that Becca's days were numbered. After we brought her home, one day Becca was sitting on the couch, cuddling with her dad. I sat down on her other side. I could not stop the silent trickle of tears down my cheek. Becca looked at my face. She turned to my husband and said, "Daddy, can I have the Kleenex?" My husband handed her the box. Becca took out a single tissue, turned to me, and gently wiped my tears away. That single gesture of love was a gift to me that I will have for the rest of my days.

Awhile after we had returned home, Becca asked to sleep in her own room. After much preparation, we brought her upstairs. She was happy to be in her bright, colorful room, filled with plush animals, artwork, and her many treasures. As always, after a "Goodnight" and "I love you," I went to sleep by her side. The next morning, I reached over to stroke her beautiful, bald head, only to find that Becca was gone. She had died peacefully in her sleep, the way of her leaving being her final miracle.

I will never forget her words: "I love rainbows because they shine in the sun. I like hearts because they are pretty. I like stars because they are up in the sky. I think flowers are beautiful because they smell good. I love the moon because it is up in the sky. I think butterflies are beautiful because they have pretty colors. I like rabbits because they are cute."

Family Miracles

BY CAROLYN SIEGEL-McGAHA

If it weren't for my father, Bernie Siegel, I might have looked at life differently. My father put my mind in a more positive direction. When we were told my son only had two to three hours left to live, I wasn't in denial; I just had so much faith in myself and a positive attitude from the start that I never gave up. My father and I were very positive and encouraging figures for Jason as well, and I believe this helped Jason to stay alive. Jason felt the powerful love, spirituality, and positive attitude that pervaded our days, and he recovered, although he continued to have health issues.

Many years later, when Jason was rushed into the hospital and placed into the ICU, the doctors were unable at first to determine what was wrong. My father was right there with the doctors and brainstormed with us, too. The doctors couldn't believe their eyes. The test results showed abnormal fatty acids and that his metabolism was off; plus, he had different types of yeasts growing in his gut and throughout his body. The doctors were able to put him on medications, and it helped them to finally diagnose him with pyruvate carboxylase deficiency.

Jason stayed in the ICU for months, asleep from his lactic acidosis and on all sorts of machines to keep him alive. When my father visited, he whispered in his ear, and Jason suddenly opened his eyes. I asked my father what he said, but he told me it was between Jason and him. "Amazing," was all I could say.

My father was also there after Jason had his brain surgery. He gave such great support. My son couldn't talk, but the day after the shunt got put in, my father got Jason to relax and stay lying down so his brain wouldn't hemorrhage. Then he spoke. He could barely talk before the surgery, and now he was saying "TV" and "Poppie!" Again, he had a miraculous recovery and went home. Jason has always looked up to "Poppie" ever since, and he gets so excited when he sees him.

My dad has been a very big support emotionally and financially with my boys. I must have called him at least five times a day asking him medical questions. My dad told me, if I wasn't his daughter, he would have sent me a bill…and we know it would have been a very, very big bill.

Not many children live past toddler years with Jason's diagnosis, and he is now twelve years old. Added to this miracle is the fact that my father taught me how to be a powerful advocate both spiritually and lovingly.

Miracle Memo

There are times when we are not capable of changing events in our lives and must leave it to God, but when we can make a difference, we are far more likely to see the result we desire happen when we step up and take responsibility for the change. When in premature labor, we look for doctors to stop the labor, but when full term we look for help in making the birth come quickly, efficiently, and produce the desired result: a healthy new life. Our efforts can make it all happen even if it has to be in God's time and not our time.

Think of the coincidence of Rich Eldredge and his first love logging onto the computer and thinking about each other at the same time. What you learn is that there are no coincidences. They also made an effort in reaching out, and for me that's where the determination comes in. You don't leave it all to some higher power to do it all for you; you participate in the birth and process of change.

C. J. Croker calls it a second chance, but the truth is they never gave up the first chance, and by keeping it alive they were reunited consciously and physically and can enjoy it in a way that unconscious and mystical connections cannot provide.

So much of the time, the miracle is turning a hardship into a blessing, as Terri Elders did. She could, if asked today, tell us why the horror she experienced as a child, and her fate of having a life-threatening illness, led her to step out into the world and teach and save lives. She understands life is difficult, and we need to step forward and heal each other with love and create more miracles.

In Heaven, as I wrote in my book *Buddy's Candle*, to help people who have lost a loved one of any species, everyone carries a beautiful candle. But if their loved ones grieve excessively, their tears put out the beloved's candle.

Becca's mom, Francine Brottman, did not do that. She treasured Becca's immortality through her love. Becca taught her mom to live and that we are not living or dying, but alive or dead, and that death comes when one is tired of one's body and ready to become perfect again by leaving the body.

Our body loves us and will do all it can to keep us alive and well as long as we love it and our life, and Becca showed that as she continued to live and create. It is no accident that she created a rainbow. Every color has meaning, and the rainbow demonstrates a life that is in order with every color and emotion in place. In his book *Cancer Ward*, Aleksandr Solzhenitsyn describes self-induced healing as a rainbow-colored butterfly.

It is also no coincidence that Becca departed her body from her bedroom. We know when it is our time to leave. I see this in drawings and patients' dreams. Purple is a spiritual color, and when a purple balloon, butterfly kite, or other object is floating up into the sky, it says, "I am ready for the spiritual transition." It was easy for Becca because she knew her family was prepared and that her love would stay with them and make her immortal. She could die next to her mom feeling the love and free of guilt.

Becca and Francine are teachers for us all. They experienced life, and Francine is left with Becca's love and immortality. Children know how to live in the moment and not in fear of the future or death.

Please love the children and help them to realize they are miracles and are capable of miracles. Then they, like the ugly duckling, don't have to do it all alone to realize they are a swan.

If you want a miracle, touch one another and express your love. Love is the only thing of permanence. It is immortal, the bridge between the living and the dead.

Get your baby pictures out
and see the miracle.

CHAPTER EIGHT

Creating Miracles

There is a bridge to the sky within your soul and a doorway to healing and peace within your heart....If we dream new realities, we will open ourselves to abundant blessings. Together we can create miracles!

— *Michael Teal*

Miracles are born of love. They are not unusual events but possibilities. Norman Cousins, an editor and writer, watched *Candid Camera* tapes and laughed himself well when suffering from a disabling type of arthritis of his spine. He wrote a book chronicling his story that became a bestseller, *Anatomy of an Illness*. As Norman Cousins documented, our bodies, minds, and spirit respond to our thoughts and feelings.

Sometimes we can create a miracle with just a smile. I always remember the woman who asked me what was wrong when I walked into her hospital room. She told me the expression on my face scared her. I told her I was thinking about how to help her, and she said, "Think in the hallway and smile when you come in here."

When you find self-love and work at achieving your potential, very different things start to happen in your life. Then you are not afraid to attempt to achieve your potential and create amazing things in your life. Some of my favorite stories deal with our potential to create miracles.

Flash: Living with Miracles

BY KAY PFALTZ

On November 2, I took Flash, my thirteen-year-old miniature dachshund, to have back surgery. I rose before dawn, trying to cast away the odd sense of foreboding, and drove the two hours to the Veterinary Referral Center. Anyone who has given his or her heart to an animal will have experienced some of the worry and anxiety as well as the love and compassion that I was feeling as I stood in the treatment room with Flash and talked to the surgeon.

Six anxious hours passed before I again spoke with her and heard the words that would shake my life. Flash did not have invertebrate disk disease, but a tumor growing on his spine. But it was what the doctor said next that would shape my sorrow: neither radiation/chemotherapy nor surgery was an option for this kind of cancer, which involved the spinal cord. Palliative care was recommended, and humane euthanasia when the pain became too great and the swelling resistant to the prednisone. She gave Flash three weeks to live, one month at the very most.

Caught off guard, grief came upon me like a wave. There followed days of anguish and deep sorrow. Grief, now indistinguishable from fear, clung to us like a cloak. Until one night.

It was about a week after we'd returned from the vet. I sat up in bed surrounded by three dogs, and in that moment there was peace. Until that moment, my mind had been a whirl of sadness and the agony of indecision. Then gently, from nowhere, a peace befell me nudging out the draining stress, and I felt profound serenity in the moment.

A state of grace.

I laughed as if a joke had just floated by. Then silence again as the soft orange glow from the salt candle blanketed the room in tranquility and warmth.

Flash breathed deeply beside me. Chance was curled next to him, offering him her quiet strength. Sasha stretched her body around him as if protecting him from further harm. In my state of grace I slipped into a moment so beautiful I was scared to move lest it leave. I remained very still…and it persisted. And again silence, except the dogs' light breathing, then… Sasha began to snore.

From that night on I decided this death sentence did not have to be our reality. I had tapped into the power of miracles; the ability to heal is within us all.

It happened slowly, but I began to change the way I understood reality: at any given moment, there was more than one outcome, and my heart was choosing the miracle. Because of a mere change in perception, my life began to transform in amazing ways.

I began to seek alternative means of healing. I sought a friend who used homeopathic, electrically charged essences, not unlike the Bach Flower Remedies. I changed Flash's diet; I supplemented with herbs and vitamins. I played Bach's Mass in B Minor and Robin Miller. But most of all I began to feel a subtle, yet powerful, "knowing."

What I now wanted, against all odds, was for Flash to be with me on Christmas day. I practiced visualization and began to see in my mind a healthy, vibrant Flash. Since I wanted Flash to see Christmas, I chose a very specific visualization. I saw him at my mother's house where we had Christmas, digging up the rug amidst scattered bits of wrapping paper. I bought three pendants, one for each of the dogs that I would open on Christmas Eve and hang on Lauren, a little white pine in my backyard. I even drew a sketch of this. As I did these things, the sense of knowing increased, and daily I was granted small signs from the universe, disguised among the plain and ordinary events of each day, validating the miracles that were happening to us now on a regular basis. Only when I woke from the "ordinary" world could I look back and see that these "miracles" had been ours all along.

I began to feel in my heart that Flash would not only see Christmas but that he would see the flowers bloom in spring. Yet I knew to remain humble and speak only to those people who would understand.

Flash made it to Christmas as I had so wanted, yet had dared not hope. And on Christmas Eve as I knelt in the ice and snow and held him in my arms to hang the three pendants on Lauren, there were tears in my eyes…but they were borne of wonder and gratitude, not sorrow. At my mother's house he dug among the discarded wrapping paper just as I had visualized, and I felt not only the joy of Christmas but quiet awe in the presence of the miracles that are ours every day.

Now it is April, and Flash is watching the flowers bloom. Where once he was stumbling and dragging his hind end, now he scampers along on our walks, eats dirt in the yard, and pokes among the tulips. And everyone says, "It's a *miracle*."

I know we are living in the grace of miracles, which I long to extend into the years ahead, a quiet assurance settling over me like comfort. But the future is not mine to decide, and the dogs have taught me not only to live in the present but to love the moment I am in. Each new day is a day to be cherished, a day that will never return to us again. And each new dawn that I turn and see him gently breathing beside me is another fluttering miracle.

Where One Surgeon Hurt — Another Surgeon Healed

BY SUSAN SNOW

I was diagnosed with stage-four cancer in April 2006 — and was given two months to live. A surgeon opened me up and found that nothing of the tumor could be removed, so my next course of treatment would be intravenous chemo and then radiation and oral chemo. After my fourth aggressive chemo treatment, I was given a CT scan to check on the cancer, and there was nothing there; it was completely gone — within the span of two months.

In December 2006, a final surgery was performed, this time by a colorectal surgeon, a different surgeon than first worked on me, and when they opened me up to remove any remaining cancer that might be there — there was none, and the results came back completely clear of cancer.

After knowing that all signs of the cancer were gone, I had to go back to that first surgeon to take out my portacath. I eagerly told him that all was well, that there was absolutely no sign whatsoever of the cancer — it was completely gone. Just when he was about to cut into me, he said, "Well, it could come back. It could go into your liver, your lungs, your pancreas." Had he not been just going to cut into me, I would have cut into him; instead I bit my lip, and when I left his office I was a complete mess. I never cried throughout my entire journey with cancer — every day I was positive, but that day a surgeon brought me to tears.

I was later told that when my family doctor and the hospital would call that surgeon for consultation from the emergency room (as I was in and out of the emergency room with severe fever and chills throughout my cancer treatments), he actually said to them on more than one occasion, "Don't bother with her; she only has two months to live."

I wanted to prove to that surgeon that what he said can kill people, that being positive can heal, and for the last four years I had been searching for someway to let him know that. You can just imagine the ideas I came up with.

Then I picked up Dr. Siegel's book — which, as it turns out, was a book that was given to me by my family doctor when I was first diagnosed with cancer. I must have lived in a cave, as I had never heard of Dr. Bernie Siegel, but there was my answer written between the pages of his book. I contacted Bernie and we exchanged emails back and forth, and from where one surgeon had hurt me with his words, another surgeon healed me through his words.

When I hit my five-year mark next year, I will send him Dr. Siegel's books and, coupled by the fact that I am still alive, maybe, just maybe, he will "get it." So, next year I will march into that surgeon's office and present him with what just might save many people's lives. Words can kill, and I truly believe that Dr. Siegel's words will heal him as well.

I now have a cancer information center on my farm, and I have put together a cancer website to give people hope and to help them find access to funding and information in everything they will be going through. Some days I question why it was that I was put through all that, and I believe it was to give others hope, and for that I am truly blessed. Miracles really do happen every day — some days we just have to look a little harder for them.

Don't Wait

BY SANDRA LEWIS

When I was younger and relatively untouched by tragedy or pain, my understanding of miracles was that they were administered randomly, by God, to people with impossible life situations. These miracles were rare — or at least very rarely reported — and never seemed to happen to anyone I actually knew. I had a neighbor dying of cancer; I knew a family whose children were a source of endless worry and trouble; a local man lost his business and committed suicide. No miracle presented itself to these people. I assumed, then, that God's mysterious ways were indeed that — mysterious — and that the chance of obtaining a miracle in one's own life was exceedingly unlikely. This was not entirely disconcerting to me, as my life was rich and full. Trouble was a stranger to me, and my life's course appeared happily set.

Six years ago, I was a homeopathic doctor, living with my husband and two children, and feeling a sense of satisfaction one feels when life runs along "as it should."

Two years later, the landscape changed forever, as one of my precious children was diagnosed with a serious, chronic disease for which conventional medicine had no acceptable solutions. I poured myself into research and scientific and holistic networking, in search of the holy grail that would remove my child from suffering and harm, and to reclaim the sense of peace and "normalcy" with which I had previously felt safely connected. With the administrations of countless remedies, supplements, special diets, and medical and alternative consultations, my child gradually improved, although symptoms remained, and with them the unrelenting threat of worse days to come. However, I slowly began to allow myself cautious optimism, which came to a shuddering halt when my other child was also diagnosed. My sense of normalcy, control, "fairness," and understanding of how the world is "supposed" to be shattered around me, and this new paradigm brought me face-to-face with who I really am, what I am really capable of, and what the world really is — and can be — about. This new reality would prove to be the beginning of a brand-new understanding, and it would joyfully remove forever the mystery surrounding "miracles."

But in the stillness, and although I was immersed in self-pity and foggy desperation, a clarity slowly dawned. Had I really used everything I had, and done everything I possibly could, to help my children heal? Or was I losing faith too early, not realizing I was on the cusp of a pivotal discovery? If miracles really existed, had I laid sufficient groundwork to create or attract such an event? I felt a burst of energy, and with it, a renewed glimmer of confidence and hope. I searched through shelves of medical and spiritual books and saw Dr. Bernie Siegel's face on one of them. Of course! I had read many of his books and knew him to be an extraordinarily wise, gifted man. Before

I lost my newfound courage, I wrote to him, telling him about my children and what I had done for them so far. I asked if there was anything he might know of that I had missed that might help set my children on a more secure path.

I felt alive again, with a new sense of empowerment, even though I was still alone in my office! Just seeing Bernie's face on one of his books reminded me that we are a global village — whether we ever meet each other or not, we are all connected, and this understanding and wisdom has the power to reignite our spirit and illuminate our greatest potentials, leading us to our greatest achievements. I didn't really expect that Bernie would personally receive my note. And so I was stunned to receive a warm reply a short while later, and with it, information and encouragement from several of Bernie's friends whom he had contacted on my behalf. The paradigm had shifted unexpectedly and profoundly.

That was just over three years ago. I had several conversations with Bernie and his friends, and over a fairly short period of time, my life was relaunched in a brilliant new direction, as I came to understand that the true miracle lies within us all. I relaunched my search for answers, breaking down walls of resistance and weaving together a myriad of opinions, research, knowledge, and experience, and I crafted a plan. My brave, loving children have been completely well for three years — there is no longer any sign of disease. Now when troubles arise (and as we know, they always do), I take hold of my inner resources, and I move with confidence and love to the best possible solution. "No" will never again be an acceptable answer.

Bernie once wrote to me, "When you are in premature labor, God steps in,...but be ready when you are full term to rebirth yourself." And so the ripple effect continues: I changed careers, wrote and published a book, and became a life coach, choosing to devote myself to helping other people solve life issues and discover their hidden power. You see, I have learned that miracles are not something we wait for. The potential for miracles continually surrounds us. The key ingredients to make those miracles happen — love, courage, and an ever-present reminder that we are all connected — all lie within us. I believe that these are the only three things we need to create miracles every day. When your heart is open to possibility and love, and you awaken your courage, you open yourself to the possibility of your own miracles, and teach others by your example.

From Chronic Pain to Marathon: The Story of My Miraculous Healing Journey

BY DR. MARK WILLIAM COCHRAN

"*On a scale from one to ten*, with one being no pain at all and ten being unbearable pain, how would you rate your pain today?"

It was the umpteenth time I had heard that question. Because of my ongoing battle with chronic pain, I had been answering it with some pretty big numbers for quite awhile. But now I decided it was time for a shift.

"Sorry, I'm not going to answer that anymore," I replied. "I'm not here for my pain; I'm here for my health." That year, 1999, I was a student at Palmer College of Chiropractic. My student doctor raised his eyebrows as I continued, "Just adjust my spine so we can turn on life! From now on, let's focus on enhancing my health and not on fighting my disease."

I wish I could tell you that after my epiphany, the clouds parted, a divine light shone down upon me from above, and I hopped off of the adjusting table and danced out the door, free of pain forever. But that did not happen. I struggled upright and shuffled out the door just as I had come in: with a slow, painful limp. Still, in that moment, with that declaration, a faint glimmer of my divine inner light began to shine through the clouds of pain, fear, and despair.

For the previous eighteen years — since age

twenty-three — I had been waging an all-out battle against inflammatory arthritis. I felt as though the pain had ruined my life. Instead of enjoying the recreational activities I had loved so much, my arthritis kept me sidelined. When I should have been rollerblading with my son, I was riding my recliner. Arthritis robbed me of joy, sleep, intimacy, and success, and it forced an early end to the Marine Corps career that I loved. In my struggle to defeat the disease, I enlisted every ally I could find: conventional medicine, herbs, chiropractic, acupuncture, past-life regression, green-lipped mussel extract…you name it. Yet, the harder I fought, it seemed, the stronger the suffering became.

As my agonizing journey progressed, I started reading the works of the healing masters of today and of bygone years. Each book benefited me and expanded my horizons in some way. The book that I found the most life-changing — the one that reached deepest into my soul and left me feeling most empowered — was *Peace, Love & Healing* by Bernie Siegel. Bernie's thoughts on self-love and inner peace guided me to turn my gaze inward, and it was there — deep inside my self — that I finally saw light at the end of my long, dark, painful tunnel.

As a chiropractic student, I had learned of the magnificent Innate Intelligence that is integral to every living being. I found wonderful teachers who helped me shift my focus from fighting pain to releasing my glorious human potential. The moment that I chose to no longer rate my pain on a scale from one to ten, I stopped fighting and began loving every aspect and manifestation of myself as a beautiful and perfect being.

Now, fast-forward to September 2005. In the midst of yet another arthritis flare-up, I woke up one morning and felt…different. I was still in pain but somehow, deep inside, I sensed that something had shifted. The new consciousness that had taken root years earlier was finally blossoming at the physical level. Over the next few weeks, my flare-up subsided far more quickly than any flare-up ever had. The following May, I entered an event in Spokane, Washington, called the Lilac Bloomsday Run. Many of the fifty thousand people who sign up for Bloomsday choose to walk the entire twelve-kilometer course. My fellow walkers and I were assigned to a separate color-coded "Lilac Group," which steps off after all the runners are on their way. As I took my place at the front of the Lilac Group, I decided to try jogging — just a little — to see how it would feel. I fleetingly toyed with the idea of trying to run a half mile, then immediately dismissed the foolish notion. "It would take a miracle," I thought, "for me to run that far."

I started jogging and felt pretty good. That first half mile came and went, and I was still running! Before I knew it, I was trotting past the one-mile marker, then the two-mile marker…and kept running for four miles before I stopped to walk for a short distance. When I crossed the finish line, I had run about six miles of the seven-and-a-half-mile event. Running across that finish line was one of the most thrilling moments of my life. It was the first time I had run four miles nonstop in over twenty-five years and the first time I had run at all in over eleven years!

I took up running again and even became a tri-athlete. The following year, at age forty-nine, I competed in two triathlons including the 70.3-mile Grand Columbian, which consisted of a 1.2-mile open water swim, a hilly and challenging 56-mile bike ride, and a sweltering 13.1-mile run. At age fifty, I took up snow-boarding and, at age fifty-one, joined a dodgeball league in which I was twenty years older than almost everyone else in the league. That's right, dodgeball! And I'm still going strong!

Do miracle cures exist? Of course they do. Right inside.

Never Say Never

BY LAURA CALLERO

I am a survivor — in the truest sense of the word. I am now fifty-one years old, married, and with three exceptional children. My story began in 1989. I was the perfect picture of health and happiness. Just married. Happy life. World travels. I had just completed law school and had a fantastic job and lots of business trips. I was in great physical shape. And then, it hit. I suffered massive backaches and headaches and was diagnosed (after two long years of misdiagnoses) with a spinal cord astrocytoma — a nine-inch tumor inside the cord itself.

I went to see Norman Cousins at UCLA and heard of Bernie from him. I read Norman's books, and Norman made me a hypnotherapy tape. I bought Bernie's books and tapes and read them and listened for hours, pre- and post-surgery. After my surgery in 1990, I was told I would be dead in three months, if that. My surgery was twelve hours long and left my right side paralyzed. I was in the hospital for nearly four months. All my friends went ahead and took the bar exam — not me. I was stuck in bed. I had to learn how to write again and how to walk.

But miracles were yet to happen. I got out of the wheelchair by sheer strength of mind, and I went and took the bar exam and passed. I went on to walk with a quad cane, and then only a brace, and now nothing. I have pain now and again, but I never say never.

I credit my survival to not giving up and the guides along my way: Bernie, Norman, and my devoted husband, Chris. Miracles *do* happen...every day...every minute. I am now a human being and not a "human doing."

The Gift of Miracles

BY STACEY CHIEW

My life experiences have helped me cultivate an awareness to make way for a deeper understanding of why miracles unfold in our lives. Some say it is nothing more than a coincidence, a matter of luck, or a question of chance. But I believe these synchronous events are here to serve us, to direct us, and to help us grow.

During the most challenging time of my life, my son was diagnosed with leukemia at the age of six. I was hoping for a cure from modern medical care. At the same time, I wanted more than conventional medicine could offer. I was looking for that missing ingredient, that missing piece of puzzle which would complete the picture. I spent some time dwelling on the causes of illness; that seemed to help a little.

I had some knowledge about alternative medicine, and it helped me regain some control of my life when my son was put on a harsh treatment regimen. But my eagerness to know more led me to a series of coincidences that ended up redirecting me and my son to the gateway of wellness.

I spent hours researching topics on cancer that might lead to cures. Be it scientific facts, natural approaches, nutrition, or a change of lifestyle, these random topics caught my eye. Only the Great Planner could have arranged such wonderful coincidences. There I was, reading the right books, talking to the right people. This series of events helped me to expand my knowledge from understanding chemotherapy to food and nutrition, from body-mind healing to energy medicine, from quantum physics to spirituality.

The stories told by Dr. Bernie Siegel were my favorite reading material. Particularly his modern presentation of esoteric knowledge that described the multidimensional nature of man using science, philosophy, psychology, and spirituality, demonstrating his profound knowledge of humanity as well as his wisdom in medicine.

Through writing to Bernie and reading his books, I was able to understand the many aspects of the body's creative intelligence and beyond. His message was simple, yet empowering: instead of holding on to a less-fulfilling life, we can all transform our lives into something meaningful. Disease, disaster, dysfunction, issues, and problems are simply the heart's inner calling to a life makeover. Bernie called it rebirth.

Bernie helped me recognize that healing is something very private, spiritual, and personal. There is no greater answer out there other than the ones we find within. There is no one-size-fits-all solution. Each one of us is having a unique experience. But when we apply the teachings that will help us and practice them, blessings happen. I realized in order to heal my son, first I must heal myself by replacing any unbeneficial thoughts or emotions with constructive ones, which would allow me and my son to live the way we want. I explored the many factors that contribute to wellness. I was aware that blame and finding fault with all kinds of things contributed nothing except adding more negative elements to our situation. They served no purpose when it came to healing a child with cancer.

So I learned to see from many different perspectives, learned how to truly listen to my son's needs, learned to trust my own gut feelings and make beneficial choices for our circumstances, and to safeguard the best interest of my son. Instead of being a fearful worrier, he became more and more courageous. He sailed through his treatment with few side effects. The treatment ended in the middle of 2009. Today he remains in good health and continues to do well in school.

Just as flowers bloom only in the sunlight, miracles involve work. They require the labor of love, the work of faith, and the patience of hope. I often see Bernie as a gift sent forth by the mysterious universe to answer what I had in mind. He was the very cool missing puzzle piece. I know this may sound strange to you, but I am looking forward to a lifetime of miracles.

Miracle Memo

These writers personify the survival behavior personality consisting of action, wisdom, and devotion. They didn't just sit there — they sought help. They know I can coach them but I can't do it for them; they have to have the desire and intention. They worked at uncovering the wisdom available to them and also had a faith in themselves and in all those involved, as well as in a higher source. They are not waiting for their luck to change, but doing the hard work to change it.

I am proud to say that from her experience, and what her dogs have taught her, Kay Pfaltz is almost as good as her dogs. First, let me say how doctors do not understand that wordswordswords become swords and can kill or cure like a scalpel. When you take hope away, you kill people who do not have the intention and desire to attempt to survive despite the predictions and statistics. When we can accept and surrender, we find peace and amazing grace.

Susan Snow understood this, that there is a potential for miracles and none of us is a statistic. Sometimes it does take work to make it happen, but what do you have to lose? Susan had the courage to say no to an authority figure and take the challenge of life and give birth to a new self. I know many patients who went home and died when they heard the same prognoses these writers did, but I also know many who got mad and were determined to exceed expectations. Most of them truly enjoy meeting doctors who gave negative prognoses and reminding them that, despite what the doctors said or believed, they are still alive.

Laura Callero is a classic case of survival behavior and how to make miracles happen. First, the action: She goes to see Norman Cousins. I always admire the people who track me, or other doctors, down from all over the world, and I tell them that they will exceed expectations because of their personality and behavior. Then, the wisdom: She reads books and listens to tapes and increases her knowledge and wisdom related to her health and well-being. Her desire and intention alter her physical state and ability, and she understands she is seeking her potential.

Sandra Lewis's family was not worried about doing it wrong and not getting better, but about their potential and what they could achieve with the right information, inspiration, and action. Guilt, shame, and blame for doing it wrong are not the issue. You step up and take a chance and live. Sandra used the problem and learned from what she was going through, then wrote her own book to help others to become strong at the broken places.

When we can accept and surrender, we find peace and amazing grace. Research has recently shown that homeopathic remedies can kill cancer cells. We are studying energy healing of cancer, and other diseases, as medical minds open to possibilities and study them instead of denying and refusing to accept them.

When Dr. Mark Cochran was in pain, and shifted from "fighting the disease," which empowers the enemy, to healing his life and body, the important change began. As Mother Teresa said, "I will not attend an anti-war rally, but if you ever have a peace rally, call me."

When I read Stacey Chiew's story, I felt it showed us that we are all potential miracles.

These writers took action and became the miracle, and they deserve the credit. It is not about failing or being disabled, but about never saying never. If we see ourselves as human beings, capable of living and loving, and not judging ourselves by comparing ourselves to others or to what is "normal," we find we are whole and complete and know it, no matter what state our bodies are in.

When people stop placing focus on worrying about statistics, they can put their energy into their potential and what they can achieve with the right information, inspiration, and action. Step up and take a chance.

*Open your mind
to all possibilities and believe!*

CHAPTER NINE

Everyday Miracles

Our true home is in the present moment. To live in the present moment is a miracle. The miracle is not to walk on water. The miracle is to walk on the green earth in the present moment, to appreciate the peace and beauty that are available now.

— *Thich Nhat Hanh*

My dear friend Elisabeth Kübler-Ross always said, "Bernie, there are no coincidences." I agree with Elisabeth wholeheartedly because we are creating our future with every decision that we make every day.

We do not meet strangers; we meet people who are destined to be on our path through life. Several years ago, after I finished writing my book *Buddy's Candle*, I was walking our dog Furphy when I heard a voice say, "Go to the animal shelter." I have learned to listen to the voice and its instructions. So down to the shelter we go. When I walked in, there was a dog sitting there, and the voice asked, "What's his name?" The answer came from a shelter volunteer: "Oh, his name is Buddy. He has been here less than fifteen minutes. The lady who adopted him didn't like his behavior." I said, "I'm here to take him home." He has been a real Buddy and loving friend.

You may dream about something tonight and see it later the next day or years from now. When you stop dreaming, you stop living. Then you have no future, and all that you will experience is the same boring repetition of the previous day. Think what could be if you only believe and have faith and hope.

Here are more of my favorite everyday miracle stories, which show us that coincidences are not just coincidences. There is a way to make the invisible visible.

Bandit, My Bolt Out of the Blue, My Miracle

BY JENNY PAVLOVIC

In January, I took my old dog, Rusty, to the vet for the last time. Rusty had been a stray, found in a neighboring state. I had adopted him from the local animal shelter, and we had been together for over seven years. Now his liver was failing, and he was very ill and in pain. Sadly, it was time to let him go.

Once the vet gave the injection and Rusty peacefully passed on, I went back out to my truck for Rainbow. She was Rusty's pal, a much younger and higher energy dog. I led Rainbow in to see Rusty, so she wouldn't wonder what had happened to him, then took her back out to the truck.

Before driving home, I was compelled to go back into the clinic to get Rainbow a chew toy. I knew she would be lonely as the only dog and would need something to keep her busy. Inside, a blue Australian cattle dog (ACD, aka blue heeler) was standing at the counter with an unfamiliar woman. I was surprised because I didn't see cattle dogs often and hadn't seen one at our vet clinic before. I asked the woman if it was okay to pet her dog. I told her that I had just lost my cattle dog mix a few minutes earlier. She encouraged me to pet the blue girl, Opal, and told me that she had a red puppy in her van. He was the last one of the litter and needed a new home. People on her waiting list had been looking for blues. I told her that I had another red heeler mix, Rainbow, in the truck and that we like the reds at our house!

I hadn't even thought about where my next dog would come from. Rusty was very old, but had only recently shown signs of illness. The woman, Louanne, told me that while she was driving to the clinic, she'd been overcome by a peaceful feeling that the red puppy would soon find his new home. She offered to bring him over to meet me. At first I resisted, telling her I couldn't make a decision on a new dog right away and that Rainbow was probably upset about Rusty passing on. I didn't know how much more emotion my heart could take that day. But Louanne brought the red pup over. To my complete astonishment, he had Rusty's double red mask and red ears.

He was a very nice, bold, playful puppy, and I was taken with him right away. He and Rainbow got along from the beginning. I didn't want to make an emotional decision, so I asked Louanne for references. Rainbow and I needed to grieve Rusty's passing. I was exhausted and needed time to think. Louanne and I exchanged information, and Rainbow and I went home. I kept thinking about that red puppy, feeling like he belonged with us. It was clear that Rainbow needed a playmate. I did my homework, contacted Louanne's references, and two weeks later Bandit joined our family.

The amazing thing is that, originally, I had made an appointment for the vet to come to my home at the end of the day to put Rusty down. But Rusty was suddenly in so much pain that I didn't want to make him wait, and I drove him to the clinic. Louanne lived over an hour away, and this was not her regular vet. She had been referred to my vet for Opal to have a special procedure, and she had brought puppy Bandit along for the ride. If I hadn't gone back in to get Rainbow a chew toy, Opal would not have caught my eye at the front counter, and I would not have met Louanne or Bandit. I believe the sequence of events that brought Bandit to me was not a coincidence. In his pain, Rusty led me to the only red ACD puppy for miles. Bandit was Rusty's gift to Rainbow and me, to help us heal from the pain of his loss. I think we experienced an everyday miracle and that Bandit was meant to be with us. My mom says that "God winked" that day.

Bandit's formal name is Hillhaven Bolt Out of the Blue. With his puppy antics and his silly rubber chicken, he brought Rainbow and me back to life. He taught me that sometimes the best friends will find you when you least expect them to, and that paying attention to them is important. Jump on a good opportunity when you see it, because life is too short and you may not get the chance again. Bandit has been a wonderful companion, a perfect fit with my personality, who has taught me so much about life. He is my bolt out of the blue, my everyday miracle, and my link back to Rusty.

On Zanussi

BY DERRICK SUTTON

As someone whose life's dream was to become a published writer, I believe the word *miracle* could sum up my chance encounter with a complete stranger in the middle of a forest — a meeting that would bring me much closer to my literary ambitions.

Before this rather strange episode, I was a complete cynic; miracles were the stuff of hocus-pocus. My steadfast skepticism sprang from seven letters that still send shivers down my spine: Zanussi.

As an eight-year-old, I had a good friend named Joe. Joe was a couple of years older than me, and so, naturally, his seniority made him an official expert on life, the universe, and everything else. Because Joe wasn't an adult, I soaked up his wisdom with a rapt attention that my teachers found wholly absent.

One summer's day we were walking back from the local shop after searching for new Spiderman comics, and this was when Joe told me in a hushed whisper about Zanussi. Zanussi, it turned out, was a planet that only children could visit; adults were barred.

Planet Zanussi had all the latest editions of all the comics in the world, and they were completely free, as were drinks, which consisted of Coca-Cola and, coincidentally, all Joe's favorite soft drinks; breakfast and dinner were minimalistic choices between chocolate, chips, or cake. In Zanussi, there was no school, and you could do whatever you wanted, whenever you wanted, imagination being the only limit.

The spaceships were leaving next weekend, and Joe asked if I was interested in coming along. I could barely breathe with excitement, let alone respond. Suddenly, the sky was so much bluer.

"What about my parents? They might not let me go…"

"Don't tell them. Don't mention Zanussi to anyone," advised Joe.

Arriving home, I managed to keep the topic of Zanussi to myself for all of twenty minutes, each second charged with the most powerful magic.

As I packed my rucksack, I kept peering up at the clouds, seven days till liftoff.

When I informed my father of my coming departure and how this might be the last time we'd see each other for a while, he revealed with no small amusement that Zanussi was a company that made electrical appliances.

After much protest and patient explanation, finally I accepted that there was no such place; I wouldn't be boarding the spaceships next weekend. My dreams of reading all the comics ever written came to a cruel and abrupt end as my belief in the miraculous fizzled away like a flat glass of free Coca-Cola.

But all was not lost.

Almost thirty years later, after I relocated to a small island in the Pacific Northwest, thousands of miles away from Britain and Joe, the bitter episode of Zanussi was laid to rest and my faith in miracles restored.

While waiting for my green card, by order of the US government, under no circumstances could I seek employment.

Ha! Jackpot!

I took to idleness like a three-toed sloth takes to hanging from branches.

After a few weeks, unadulterated idleness lost its appeal. I shed the all-day pajamas, my erratic hairstyle (which was last in fashion when our ancestors used entrails to divine their futures), and took up an online course in Internet marketing.

I have no idea why, but I found the subject absolutely fascinating.

My wife had an online jewelry store, so I started to apply some of the lessons to her shop, and soon it began to rank really well with the search engines.

As soon as my government-enforced idleness was lifted, I wrote and sold a series of ebooks to help other artists market their work online. These sold with moderate success and some terrific reviews. I was over the moon!

One day, my wife and I went for a walk in a nearby forest with my visiting aunt. The woods consisted of a huge network of paths and trails with deceptively gentle names like "Wuthering Heights" (an almost vertical climb and place of unspeakable horror for recovering idlers).

Suddenly, out of the blue (or perhaps the imagination of Jim Henson), a gangly, animated hound appeared on the trail, followed by his master.

"What sort of dog is that?"

We got talking and I discovered I was in the company of a fellow writer. This was quite the coincidence; the forest was huge, and aside from the odd chipmunk and slug, we hadn't seen another soul on our journey. We swapped details and he invited me to his writers group.

He explained that "Just Write" had been generously founded by a literary agent, keen to help others expand their writing and creativity.

There is a unique and miraculous power that can fill you when you surround yourself with people who share your hopes, dreams, and passions; with a newfound energy, I began work on a novel.

This was where the final pieces fell into place.

Within a few weeks of joining "Just Write," I received an email from an editor with an international publishing company. They'd seen my ebooks and expressed interest in publishing them; the editor asked me if I had an agent...

The answer was no, but I knew who to ask!

Being a published writer was something I'd dreamed of all my life, but prior to this, I had no clue when it came to the protocols of dealing with publishers or how to find a literary agent.

If it hadn't been for that serendipitous ramble

in the woods and a gregarious dog that inspired a chance meeting, I may never have found this wonderful opportunity.

My faith in the miraculous had been restored: I had found Planet Zanussi.

Homeward Bound

BY ANNMARIE B. TAIT

No six-year-old awaiting Santa was ever more excited than I was with every item I placed into the suitcase. After spending two years at the Centerville Beach Naval Facility in Ferndale, California, my husband, Joe, and I were heading home to the East Coast, but a quick hop home on a jet just wasn't for us. We planned a three-thousand-mile sightseeing road trip the likes of which would bring a tear to the eye of every auto club TripTik map plotter on earth.

Back in 1986 our assets were limited to youth, enthusiasm, and a positive attitude. On the other hand, our liabilities boasted length and girth.

Heading the list was our Pontiac LeMans, whose heyday peaked around the same time Neil Armstrong took one giant leap for mankind. But the LeMans was reliable — ugly, faded, lacking air conditioning and a radio, but reliable. She earned the reliability badge two years prior when we drove her cross-country the first time. But our first trip was hurried, and this time we were determined to enjoy every inch of terrain between California and Philadelphia.

With youth, enthusiasm, and that positive attitude taking up most of the room in the back seat, caution took a flying leap right out the window. So, off we rolled onto Route 101 South. First stop, San Francisco and the Napa Valley where Ghirardelli

Chocolates, Fisherman's Wharf, and vineyards galore stood to make a tidy profit indeed on this, our last hurrah before returning home.

We were on the road only about three hours when the LeMans began to develop an allergic reaction to land formations of an uphill nature. She didn't actually refuse to climb; she just sort of coughed her way to the top of an incline, then wheezed clear down the other side. The further we drove, the harder it was for her to get us from one side of a hill to the other.

When we reached San Francisco, we checked in to our hotel, but the gray cloud of the engine that "couldn't" threw a damper on the first leg of our long-awaited journey in a big way. Several repair attempts were thwarted by mechanics who could not duplicate the symptoms on a road test, creating quite an ominous mystery that worsened the longer we drove each day.

Enter Plan B. To minimize inconveniencing other drivers on the imminent mountain passes ahead, we decided to do most of the heavy driving during the wee hours. Every day we started out at about 1 AM and drove until about 8 AM. Then we found a place to stay, took in the local sites, got a bite to eat, and went to sleep around 4:30. At about midnight the party started all over again.

Our grip on the positive attitude slipped with every incline we limped over. But hope? We trapped hope in a full nelson lock. Never was this more apparent than early one morning, nearing Reno. A steep incline loomed ahead on Route 80, and a peppy little RV gained on us from behind. Right then we hoped with all our might that the driver would back off. Instead, he inched ever closer. Finally we reached a shoulder in the road and pulled to the side with a sigh of relief, fully expecting to see the driver pass us with all speed, leaving in his wake a less-than-friendly gesture or two.

Much to our surprise and increased anxiety, the driver stopped behind us, then stepped out of his RV and headed in our direction. All I could think of was how long it might take the Highway Patrol to find our bodies and how he would fake the accident. Imagine my relief when I noticed him smiling. Believe it or not, this gentleman, who introduced himself as Tom, was a retired Pontiac design engineer who happened to be one of the original designers of the Pontiac LeMans.

According to our new best friend Tom, the Pontiac LeMans operated with a fuel system that engaged two gas lines. One hose carried fuel to the engine; the other siphoned off the excess back to the tank. This saved fuel. It worked like a charm for years but deteriorated with age, and now the siphon hose was inadvertently sucking back most of the fuel needed to fire the engine up an incline.

As Tom calmly explained the problem, I envisioned us boarding a Greyhound bus with all our belongings strapped to our backs, minus our abandoned enthusiasm and positive attitude.

I am delighted to report that Greyhound sold no tickets to us that day. In less than five minutes Tom crawled under the car and plugged the second gas line with a pencil, then shimmied his way back out and assured us our hill climbing disasters were over. We stood there with our mouths hanging open — stupefied by the whole sequence of events.

I wanted to pay him, take him to breakfast, walk his dog, something — anything — but Tom wouldn't hear of it. He just laughed and said he would follow us for a bit to make sure we were okay.

As promised, Tom stayed close behind us until we reached the downgrade. Then we pulled over and let him pass. He smiled and waved as he drove by, and we beeped our horn in thanks.

Happily, we rolled all the way home, over hill and dale with nary the slightest hesitation. Along the way we enjoyed Yosemite National Park, Mount Rushmore, and countless other sights that would have all been sacrificed had Tom not appeared in our rearview mirror.

I don't imagine this event registers very high on the Richter scale of miracles except in our lives, but I'm pretty sure it does register. In fact, I'm a little amazed I didn't see little wings flapping off the back of Tom's bumper as he rolled past and waved good-bye.

Miracle Memo

When we create a quiet life and a quiet mind, we can listen to our true selves, and then the path we need to follow to create the life we were intended to live will be revealed. Jenny Pavlovic, in her story about Bandit, responded to her inner feelings and grief over the loss of her dog, and she was guided to what was meant to be — meeting and adopting Bandit from a total stranger.

Derrick Sutton needed to have faith in Zanussi, and eventually he found it through his journey along the path of his life. His miracle happened because he never really stopped dreaming. When Derrick stayed open, a whole new world opened up. It is not an accident to meet your guide on a path you are taking, be it real or spiritual. When you follow your heart, magic happens. As Yogi Berra said, "When you come to a fork in the road, take it."

Annmarie B. Tait and the driver who helped her and Joe were in the right place consciously, so they made it all possible. In fact, I would say that Tom showing up was related to the journey Annmarie and Joe were on, and despite their car problems they did not lose track of the joy of their journey and life.

I had a similar experience when being driven to the airport through a deserted stretch of the Midwest and getting a flat tire. The woman driving us said she had no jack, as her husband had taken it out of the car. So there we sat, prior to the cell phone era, stuck in the middle of nowhere. But who should appear a minute later? A young man in a pickup who replaced the flat faster than I ever could have with all the right equipment. And off we went and made our plane with no difficulty.

*Quiet your mind, listen for the voice,
do what feels right, look for signs to direct you,
and watch how the coincidences and
miracles start happening.*

CHAPTER TEN

Meditation and Visualization

And the miracle is: if you can go into your suffering as a meditation, watching, to the deepest roots of it, just through watching, it disappears.

— *Osho*

The mind is all-powerful, and what it truly believes, happens. There is a greater power that needs to be believed in and explored, so that it can be accepted and accessible to us all. I think the mind's ability to believe and connect with this power is not a simple intellectual task, but one that involves our consciousness and true sense of being.

Our body doesn't need instructions on how to live in a physical sense, but it does need the right messages — to be aware of our feelings and our state of consciousness. Meditation is a method by which we can stop listening to the everyday pressures and distractions of our lives so that we may instead acknowledge the products of our unconscious mind: our deeper thoughts and feelings, spiritual awareness, and the peace of pure consciousness.

Meditation is hardly a passive process, as we actively focus our minds in a state of relaxed awareness. I meditate each day, and I take it as an opportunity to focus on the blessings, rather than the problems. I remind myself that I am grateful to be alive in order to have the problems I do! This is, indeed, an active form of gratitude.

We meditate in order to be in touch with the dreams and images God speaks through and uses to communicate with us about the spiritual and somatic truths in our lives we need to be aware of. Meditation is not just about quieting the mind; it is about freeing the collective consciousness so it can share its wisdom about our past, present, and future.

Guidance and practice in meditation can lead to phenomenal experiences of cosmic at-oneness and enlightenment. In fact, I don't know of any other activity that can reprogram our systems and improve the quality of our lives to such a great degree. Meditation and visualization benefit us physically, psychologically, and spiritually. There are no limits to the guidance that comes from within, to connect us to the greater consciousness of creation.

The stories in this chapter demonstrate the power of meditation and visualization, and the miraculous effects they can have in a person's life.

Miracle of Pain Relief

BY LISA OAKS

At thirty-one years old, I was an athletic woman who gardened for relaxation. I not only worked full-time but had strength and energy for anything in life. I was the first woman hired at the truck rental company where I worked, and because I wore so many hats as an accounts receivable and payable problem solver, they piled on the work. I met every challenge.

As I was putting an appliance dolly into a twenty-four-foot truck, I felt a violent earthquake down my entire spine. I dragged my left leg for six weeks waiting to hear back from the doctor. My foot was gray and purple, and I would fall down at work because of the numbness in my leg.

When the MRI finally came back, I was told I needed emergency spine surgery. My husband and I were stunned. More procedures followed. After two spine surgeries, I needed a wheelchair and a walker, which I despised. I was paralyzed for a week and a half from the waist down and was sent home from the ER with sinus spray Stadol, forcing my husband and mother to keep me sedated and take care of all my functions. Although I was in hell, I had my faith, my husband, and my mother to keep me hopeful.

Since the pain medications were not controlling the severe pain, I would get a morphine shot and a different bottle of pills on my visits to the hospital

— which for a while averaged every three days. Finally, I wandered into a mega-bookstore looking for a self-hypnosis tape to save my sanity and found Bernie Siegel's *Meditations for Morning and Evening*. Dr. Siegel instructed me on how to take a journey outside my body in my mind to my favorite spot. I was a complete novice, having never used meditation or self-hypnosis before. By following Dr. Siegel's instructions to build a bridge to my favorite spot and smell the air and hear the sounds — to look at the colors — I was able to transcend my pain-ridden body. And when I returned from my favorite place, I always felt so relaxed — every muscle, every nerve. I felt free for hours afterward, which is priceless when you live with chronic pain.

It saved my life because I could leave my body, destroyed with pain and debilitation, and take a journey, truly transcend. When I came back, I felt relaxed and empowered that I would fully control how my body and mind react to chronic severe pain.

I'm forty-three years old now, and I have worked extremely hard at physical therapy. It took seven long years to stop dragging my leg and foot, and I have not been able to return to work. I can now walk for approximately an hour and a half, sometimes more, with a sit-down break. This Christmas was the first time in three years that I decorated my tree, and it was a joy. There is no cure for severe damage to the spinal cord and surrounding muscles, but I will never give up hope. Every day that I feel like doing something, I do it to the point of level-ten pain and dragging my leg again, but it's worth the sense of pride I feel. I still use Dr. Siegel's meditations of deep breathing, relaxing my body, and going to my favorite spot in my mind.

Power of the Mind

BY TINA BRANNON

At age fourteen, I was diagnosed with stage-three Hodgkin's disease and given three months to live. Three months became thirty-four years. I have defied the odds, not once, but twice, as I have recently beaten stage-three breast cancer.

I chose to believe in a power greater than cancer. I believe in God and the power of prayer. I believe in miracles and love that heals. I believe the mind is powerful beyond measure. I used my mind all my life as an athlete. I used visual imagery before I knew it had a name. I used it to visualize the pitch of a soft-ball and the crosscourt or backhand of a tennis ball. I would visualize where I aimed before the ball left my hand. I would pause to visualize where I wanted the ball to land. I believed in having a vision, knowing what one wanted, and then following that vision into realization.

I was in eighth grade when I realized I could utilize visualization to fight cancer. I heard my nurses discussing a surgeon named Bernie Siegel. I was in the hospital waiting to begin emergency radiation treatment to decrease a grapefruit-sized tumor that was displacing my trachea and obstructing my airway. They stood just outside my hospital room discussing the surgeon with praise. I recall the nurses describing the mental visual of a battle between light and dark, good and evil. It was a miracle that I even heard the nurses' discussion.

I immediately set the eagle in motion against the evil cancer cells that I envisioned as snakes. The eagle was my warrior that soared gracefully above all. I saw in my mind the eagle diving and shredding the snakes one at a time. I envisioned the battle constantly while lying in the hospital bed, going through X-rays, lab work, brutal experimental chemotherapy, and radiation treatment. The war was so vivid in my mind. In the end, the eagle conquered.

Five years later, I looked up the surgeon and his work. I loved everything I learned about Bernie. I recall interviews and followed all his work, as I was in a medical career, giving back. Working with cancer patients all my life, I suggested Bernie's resources and would teach patients about the power of the mind and Bernie's technique.

Little did I know, I would employ Bernie's works again, thirty-four years later to help fight breast cancer. I used the same battle in my mind over and over. I haven't stopped.

As an athlete, nurse, patient advocate, founder of a nonprofit, photographer, and author, I have been blessed with the opportunity to inspire many through my story of faith and healing. In photography, I use the frame of a camera to capture moments. In athletics, I could use my shyness to concentrate and focus on the sport. I ended college with a BS in biology and worked in nursing and medical business. I helped build the first freestanding oncology center in

Oklahoma and went from there to start Oklahoma Cancer Care Foundation, providing cancer patients with transportation to and from treatment. I have served in medicine for about thirty years and continue to serve as a cancer coach through my foundation, helping people navigate the medical maze of oncology.

When we share, we inspire and we heal. As we heal, the world heals. I believe our triumph over adversity, ultimately, is our gift to the world.

Miracle Memo

When we listen to ourselves and others, we get to know who we are. Consciousness is a part of all these miracles and does not require a physical body to exist. Consciousness is a part of us and is immortal.

I always remember being at a conference with Louise Hay, and when someone with an autoimmune disease stood up, Louise asked her what anger she was dealing with that needed to be expressed. The reason for Lisa Oaks's success story lies within her and not with me or the CDs or books purchased. I can only coach my patients and listeners. I cannot cure them. These writers may have listened to my voice and been guided by my words, but they still had to do the work and create the miracle. I have learned that I am simply a coach, but I also know that when people are willing to participate and show up for practice, some winners are created.

For example, Tina Brannon's athletic ability helped her to survive, and not just because of the health benefits of exercise and the fact that cancer patients who exercise do better, but because of the state of mind athletes have. Lance Armstrong's survival is not a coincidence. He knew he had to show up for practice and visualize and rehearse in order to make things happen as he desired them to happen. It can help when one is also an artist or photographer because those who are visual people will get more from the visualizations than an auditory or tactile person, unless they incorporate sounds and touch into their visualization exercises.

Let consciousness speak to you of the wisdom within through meditation.

CHAPTER ELEVEN

The Power of Prayer

The value of consistent prayer is not that He will hear us, but that we will hear Him.

— William McGill

Miracles happen because they are a part of our potential. I do not expect them; I rely on them. When you have faith and believe, then miracles happen. That can be faith in the Lord or faith in your medical treatment. I know of people whose tumors shrank when they thought they were being treated with radiation when no one was aware the machine was broken, and they weren't receiving any radiation.

Miracles are built into the system, and our consciousness and energy fields affect others. I have been healed by the touch of a healer and able to rescue a missing animal in Connecticut with the words of my animal-intuitive friend in California, who said, "The cat is alive. I can see through her eyes." I know people who have cured cancer with their energy and are being studied now. Minds are opening to the world of miracles and the unexplained more than ever before. There have been focused studies that showed patients who were prayed for did better than those not prayed for.

I have helped people to die, telling those who were declared brain dead and in a coma for years that their love will stay with their family, and if they needed to go, it was all right. Within minutes these people have died because we can hear when asleep, in a coma, or anesthetized.

Now if our consciousness can make these decisions, then perhaps prayer can affect the outcome, too. Studies have shown that it can, and quantum physicists relate that a prayer is more likely to help when it is not specific but more of a blessing for the person.

In the stories in this chapter, Marsi Meli used both prayer and visualization to make a miracle possible; Kayla Finlay's prayer led to action; Marilyn Holasek Lloyd learned about the power of prayer in large numbers; Annmarie B. Tait's mother proved that perseverance in prayer can work miracles; and Heather Murphy had faith in the sign that guided her to pray.

Prayer Miracles: Against the Odds

BY MARSI MELI

In April 2005 my father had recovered from a heart attack and a triple bypass. My mother became worn down and tired from the experience of caring for my dad. My mother also has lupus, so we thought her exhaustion was the lupus rearing up its head. My dad left the house to go grocery shopping; I was home on vacation from work. It was a Friday. About fifteen minutes after my father left, my mother cried out to me, "My stomach is on fire." I went to her and she grabbed my hand. "I am going to die," she said to me. My mother has a very high pain tolerance, so for her to cry out like that was very serious. I called an ambulance.

My mother was barely conscious; her eyes were rolled back. The doctor pulled me out of the room and asked me if I realized what was happening. I responded, "She's dying." He told me my mother was the sickest person in the hospital, they had to operate, and I was to gather my family and to pray.

Surgery showed that my mother had colon cancer and fecal peritonitis. The cancer was considered a secondary concern; the peritonitis was the danger. Her chances of survival were low. She was already weak when this happened, and she had a lifelong use of steroids (because of the lupus) that would slow healing. The doctor told us we should expect the best but prepare for the worst.

My mother was on a ventilator. There was a tube through her nose that the remaining sludge in her system was coming out of. When I was in the room with her, and she was barely conscious, I put my hands over her and said to her, "Mom, you are surrounded by a white light. The light is pure positive energy and love. That light is around you and protects you. It is flowing through you. It is healing you; it is purging you of the poisons in your body; it is healing your incisions; it is keeping you strong and repels all virus and infection. You are loved." I noticed when I did that the sludge in the nose tube would start rushing out.

I told my sister Lori about it. She went in to my mother, and when she came out to me, she said, "I said the Lord's Prayer over her and it did what you said!"

One day a nurse came out and told my family, "I don't know what you are doing, but keep it up. Your mother is fighting this." The nurse then told me at night that she and other nurses would stand around my mother, join hands, and pray.

My mother did get stronger. She got off the ventilator, and the tube was removed from her nose. She was taken out of critical care and, after a stay in a rehab, was finally home. By November 2005, she started chemo for stage-four colon cancer.

It is now coming up on her five-year anniversary, and my mother is still going strong. Every time I get the feeling of being overwhelmed and that so much is against me, I remember watching my mother grow strong and beat overwhelming odds to survive. That was a miracle.

Miracles in the Moments of Life

BY KAYLA FINLAY

In fall of 1997, life as I knew it screeched to a halt as I was driven to my knees in a way my previous life's challenges hadn't been able to do. It's not as if losing my first two children to premature births and deaths a year and a week apart in 1972–73 hadn't prepared me for what was to become several years of extraordinary medical situations for myself and for my subsequent children.

Yet, only a few months after caring for a father with a terminal brain tumor during his transition from life to death, while at the same time caring for a mother with Alzheimer's, I got the news that one of my beloved children had just received a diagnosis of familial adenomatous polyposis/Gardner's syndrome (FAP/GS) at the tender age of twenty-one.

I knew nothing of this rare, genetic form of hereditary colon cancer. Yet with the help of the Internet, I learned more than I'd ever wanted to know about this life-threatening and quality-of-life-altering disease, for which there is presently no cure. There was no comfort to be found in researching FAP/GS. There were no success stories, only "nightmares that no one knows about." The diagnosis was so serious and life-threatening, we succumbed to the immediate pressure of the doctors and hospitals to have my child's large intestine removed. True to form for FAP/GS, it was blanketed with adenomatous polyps, which all become cancerous if left alone.

Within weeks of the diagnosis, I was sitting at the bedside of my barely adult child, praying for a miracle.

Meeting Laura Szabo-Cohen was my miracle. Her child had the same rare disease. During the next few weeks, in an attempt to feel we were doing something in the name of helping our children, we cofounded Garden Voices, Inc., a nonprofit dedicated to offering online, telephone, and emotional support to families who were in the belly of the beast with this disease.

Initially, we were heartbroken and in shock at the medical reality suddenly placed in our midst. We could barely wrap our minds around the prognosis and invasiveness of tests and procedures facing our young adult children. As we shared and talked with other families in online support groups for FAP/GS, we struggled to hold on to a hope for any kind of future that involved a stable quality of life for our children or others with this disease.

After two major surgeries, my child decided to deal with life with the intention of making quality of life more important than quantity of time spent here on earth. The choice to not have every suggested invasive testing procedure was my child's brave decision, one arrived at by listening to personal inner wisdom and Divine Intelligence. It was a conscious choice and one that opens all options for healing.

Laura's son chose the more traditional Western

medical route, one that resonated with his inner voice and wisdom. Both of our children have a wisdom and spirit far surpassing their chronological age, and I know their souls were elevated even before their earthly experience with FAP/GS. Neither has allowed the harsh reality of this disease to define them. I continue to be humbled to have them both in my life.

A Lesson in the Power of Prayer

BY MARILYN HOLASEK LLOYD

This past fall, I was given a life lesson in the power of prayer. My friend, Barbara, had a recurrence of cancer of the small intestine. It had spread to her liver and had destroyed two of her heart valves. In this debilitated condition, she would need open-heart surgery to replace two valves and put in a pacemaker. Luckily, she was in good hands. Experts were found for this condition, although we heard only fourteen people in the world had had this treatment and survived.

The day of her surgery, our wellness group — originally started by Barbara, which included survivors of cancer and physical abuse who were trying to stay well — was on high alert, waiting for news and praying (which was all we could do). The first news was great, surgery progressing nicely, but then we heard nothing. Finally, her husband called and said that when they went to close up her chest, her heart failed, so they had to send her to intensive care.

During the whole ordeal, Barbara's family was incredible. They never left her side, encouraging her, talking to her, loving her. All they asked for from the rest of us were more prayers.

That evening, I was so upset that I began to reach out to people I hardly knew. I was on my husband's cancer listserv site and noticed there was a priest,

Father Bill, who lived in New Orleans. I'm not Catholic, but I reached out to him and asked him to pray for my friend, Barbara. The next day he said several masses for her.

Barbara had people praying for her all over the country, and we considered everything that happened to her a miracle. After four days lying there with an open chest, Barbara had her chest closed up and her heart did well. She did not get an infection and was out of intensive care in a few days. She left the hospital a week later and stayed in a Residence Inn for five weeks with her husband, mother, and adult children at her side.

She returned to Fredericksburg after being gone six weeks. She continues to do well, and her heart is now beating on its own (with the pacemaker working as only a backup), which even the doctors couldn't believe. At the present time, Barbara is walking three miles a day.

When I had a chance to ask Barbara more about what she remembered from her time in intensive care, cold chills went through my body. The entire time she was in the intensive care, she kept saying to her family, "Who's playing that zydeco music?" They would answer her, "I don't hear any music." Now the fact that Barbara, under sedation, was hearing music was not a surprise. Barbara is a jazz singer. She sang with the Big Band in Fredericksburg for twenty years, with Sweet N Jazzy. But I really didn't know what zydeco music is. She told me that zydeco music is a "combination of Cajun and Creole music that evolved into zydeco music found only in Southwest Louisiana." I immediately thought of Father Bill who lives in New Orleans and what he did for Barbara. Was it just a coincidence that of all the music in the world, she heard this particular type?

Certainly this falls within the realm of the sixth sense or even in the realm of miracles. Who can explain such a phenomena? But I don't care to explain it; I'm grateful that our friend, Barbara, survived something now fifteen people in the world survived, and she is back with her family and friends making the most of every day. I learned again what the power of prayer can do.

Battle Plans

BY ANNMARIE B. TAIT

In early June 1968 the excitement of school letting out for the summer fizzled in the shadow of my brother's army enlistment during the height of the Vietnam War. Back then I was in the fifth grade and the youngest of five children that numbered four girls and one boy.

Many were the days at Holy Cross Elementary School when we kids attended the funeral of a classmate's brother killed in action. We prayed daily for the recovery of former parish altar boys and choirboys wounded in action. In January, 205 Americans were killed in the battle of Khe Sanh, and another 119 were lost in February at the battle of Hue. It was a grim year, and one I remember well.

So, on the morning of June 12, 1968, when my brother Bobby left for Fort Bragg, North Carolina, teary-eyed good-byes were the featured event. These were not the usual "You're going off on your own and we'll miss you like crazy" sentimental tears — the kind shed for siblings setting out for college dorms, or getting married. These were "Oh my gosh, this is *war* and you could wind up dead!" — sobs mightily weighed down by gruesome nightly newsreels and morbid photos spread throughout the pages of *Life* magazine.

As we girls sobbed and sighed, Mom stood her

ground and never shed a tear, at least none that I ever saw. My mother was no stranger to the fear that war imparts, for she was a World War II veteran herself. Mom enlisted with the first class of US Women Marines in 1943. "Free a Man to Fight" was the poster slogan that drew her to the recruiting office. Clearly against her own mother's wishes, she followed her heart and enlisted for love of country. Stationed in Washington DC, my mother attained the rank of sergeant in the US Marine Corps Women Recruits, first class. In those days military regulations prevented women from engaging in battle, but she ended up with a front-row seat to the aftermath and tragedy that war inflicted on one family after another.

Even with all her background and experience, Mom stood stoic with full faith that Bobby would return home one day unharmed — though her military training was not the well from which she drew her strength. Mom invested her faith in a higher authority, and like any good marine, she had a battle plan. The only thing the rest of us had was the reality of Walter Cronkite's nightly casualty count, which hit far too close to home for us every time we heard about another Philadelphian kid who would never return to Mt. Airy to dribble a basketball.

Off we went to school, and as the day progressed I imagined the possibility of Bobby's photo being added to the memorial wall in our school foyer. It was a sobering thought, and I pushed it out of my mind every time it snuck in.

Later that evening we ate dinner, doing our best

to ignore the hole at the table where just the night before my six-foot-five-inch clown-of-a-brother sat hurling remarks at his four sisters in his usual wise-cracking style. In somber silence we toyed with the food on our plates until Mom began clearing the table.

Just as we started heading out of the kitchen to tackle our homework, my mother ordered an "about face." With very little fanfare, she pulled her old wooden rosary beads out of her apron pocket and promptly announced that we would say the rosary together every night for the duration of boot camp. We would pray that God would spare my brother from active duty in Vietnam. In return God would answer our prayers. Of this she had absolutely no doubt.

Right then I was sure my mother had officially lost her mind. I knew of no one from our neighborhood who enlisted and escaped Vietnam — no one. And did she really think I was going to kneel down on the cold hard kitchen floor every night for the next twelve weeks to say the rosary...*out loud*? What if my friends walked by and heard the lot of us praying *out loud*? It just wouldn't work for a fifth grader. It wasn't cool. It was wimpy and weird, as a matter of fact. I mean, concern for my brother was one thing, but I saw no reason to turn into religious fanatics over the whole event. But, Mom had a plan, and it was clear from the look on her face that I had no choice.

So, on the first night of my brother's enlistment we all knelt together in the kitchen on the cold hard floor and recited the rosary. Then we did it the next night, and the next, until one day in September when my brother called right after his boot camp graduation ceremony.

The call came around dinnertime, and we were all close at hand. Mom answered the phone and her beaming smile made easy work of figuring out who she was talking to. They didn't talk long. All we heard on our end was "Yes, yes…I'll tell them right away… Take care of yourself…bye-bye." She hung up the phone, and for the first time since my brother left home, Mom cried.

We said the rosary again that night, but this time we said it in thanksgiving. My brother's entire platoon was headed for Vietnam — with the exception of two recruits. Bobby and one other private were assigned to special duty in northern Italy, where he spent the duration of his enlistment.

Such was the power my mother had with the Lord. She never wavered for one moment when it came to seeking a miracle, no matter what the odds were. She was relentless with prayer. Sometimes I think God gave in just so she would change the subject. My mother always was a marine with a battle plan — that usually started with her old wooden rosary beads.

A Motley Crew of Angels

BY HEATHER MURPHY

The not-so-funny joke in my family was that my family members had the bad habit of dying during the weeks I took vacation. My grandfather, grandmother, great-aunt, and father had all died over a period of years, but each while I was enjoying some time off from work. My brother said he was going to wear a bucket on his head when I vacationed, just to be on the safe side.

So when I learned my sister, who lived in Florida, was having knee surgery during a week I was going to be vacationing in Charleston, South Carolina, I suggested she reschedule. When she refused, I made a point to put the date and time of her surgery on my calendar and asked that my administrative assistant do the same. We made a promise to pray for my sister at the appointed time.

Of course, once on vacation, I was completely in the moment and enjoying exploring the city. Praying for my sister's surgery was the farthest thing from my mind, when suddenly I was gripped with the sensation of being unable to breathe. I told my husband I was struggling to breathe, and he said, "No, you're not. You are breathing and talking just fine."

Almost immediately, my young son came running out of a nearby bookstore. "Mom," he cried. "I can't breathe!"

I looked from him to my husband, then back to him. "Kevin, you are breathing fine," I said. "But what is going on?"

"Someone can't breathe!" I thought. And then it dawned on me what day and time it was. "Quick," I said. "We have to pray for Aunt Peggy." I gathered my family together, joined hands, and prayed for the safety and well-being of my sister. "Heal her, God. Protect her, God. May the angels and archangels and all the company of heaven be with her and keep her safe and, if need be, help her breathe," I prayed. The sensation of being unable to breathe passed from both me and my son as soon as I said the words.

Back in North Carolina, Glenda was taking a break when she glanced at her calendar. "Oh!" she thought. "I almost forgot." She, too, then bowed her head and prayed for my sister's health.

Meanwhile, in Florida, my sister was in trouble. Unbeknownst to me, she had rescheduled the surgery for the week before but hadn't told me, for fear I'd think I really was a jinx. But an unforeseen complication — an embolism — was now threatening her life. As she struggled to breathe, the doctors were trying to convince her that placing a screen in front of her heart was her only chance for survival, and it was extremely risky. Her husband was being prepared for the worst. My sister was defiant that she did not want the surgery, even as she gasped for breath.

Later my sister would describe suddenly seeing a room full of concerned people surrounding her. She did not recognize a face in the crowd, which looked to be made up of homeless street people dressed in rags, with dirty hands and faces. But they seemed to be genuinely concerned for her welfare, and she watched them carefully as they muttered things she couldn't hear or understand. Their sweet eyes were filled with compassion, almost sadness.

As suddenly as they had appeared, they were gone. At that point, my sister gasped for air, sat up, and said she felt much better. The doctors examined her in disbelief, only to find that the life-threatening blood clot had dissolved.

Her miracle cure came at exactly the same time my assistant, my family, and I had asked for intercessory prayer — and it had even come with a psychic nudge in the form of our own breathlessness!

This motley crew has since shown up on other occasions — angels whose only apparent home is where the healing is.

Miracle Memo

Consciousness is not limited to the human body, and our state of consciousness affects those we have relationships with. Prayer and love have powerful effects. Quantum physicists and astronomers deal with this every day. They don't have all the answers, but they understand that desire and intention alter the physical world, causing things to occur that would not normally occur if they were not desired. I had a patient's heart stop beating during an operation. The anesthesiologist and I did all we could, but his heart did not respond. So, with nothing to lose, I said, "Donald, it's not your time yet. Come on back." His heart started beating again and he recovered completely.

Marilyn Holasek Lloyd kept an open mind and had the courage to reach out and seek help for her friend through prayer. Even the nurses joined in, and results were miraculous, beyond the doctors' expectations.

As I have said, there are no coincidences, so the zydeco music Marilyn's friend Barbara heard was connected with the consciousness and prayers directed to her to help heal. I really think we sleep in order to get in touch with this inner wisdom. In her coma her body could speak to her through images and words and the universal consciousness.

Intention and prayer can alter the physical, and when you add determination and desire, that is when miracles happen. Annmarie B. Tait's mother did all these things, and her son was divinely protected. Faith leads to inner peace and healing.

Heather Murphy and her family and friends all prayed for Aunt Peggy to breathe and be safe. They didn't pray that her embolus dissolve, and yet the prayer worked. I believe it is the nonlocal nature of love and prayer that can make a difference. I know that every prayer does not result in achieving what the praying person wants, but that is a whole other story and it is not about our being failures or praying inadequately but that there is a time to live and a time to die. However, I think the more we accept and explore the nature of energy, love, and prayer, the more we will begin to understand our potential, divine nature, and miracles.

Let go of trying to control what isn't yours
to control to begin with.

CHAPTER TWELVE

Holiday Miracles

Blessed is the season which engages the whole world in a conspiracy of love.

— *Hamilton Wright Mabie*

Holidays can be a stressful time and a joy-filled time, but it always seems to be a season when miracles abound.

I grew up Jewish, but for me Santa did not have a religion, nor did the Easter Bunny. My wife grew up with a Christmas tree in her home, but we did not have one in our house. So we shared gifts over many holidays and combined Hanukah gifts and candles with Santa's visit.

I am reminded of my childhood in Brooklyn, New York, where I shared days off from school with my friend Carmine. His house was very different, with Jesus in the living room, but we were all family;

I would stay home on his holidays and he would stay home on mine. Our parents did not know we were taking extra days off from school. It was our thing.

One morning, I had a delicious breakfast at Carmine's house, which included bacon. When I recommended it to my Orthodox Jewish grandfather, I thought he was going to faint. Fortunately, we were all family, so there was no conflict over what happened. However, if I do not get to Heaven, you will all know it was the bacon that did me in.

The Christmas holidays are a permanent reminder to me of the power of the mind. When we learned my wife was going to have twins and was due to deliver in December, I started trying to calculate when they would be born based upon the numerical system she had worked out — like our first being born on the twenty-third, which is the sum of our birthdays, nine plus fourteen — until she said to me, "I will not be in the hospital on Christmas." Then I knew what to expect, and sure enough, the twins were born on December 26. As we sat and listened to the Christmas carols being played, we decided to name our daughter Carolyn and our son Keith.

I had fun playing Santa at the local school our kids attended. Having five children, I knew almost all the children and their families. I would walk into the classroom dressed as Santa and start giving specific advice and directions to the kids by name: "Sam, if you do not stop bothering your brother, there will be no gifts this year." The looks on their faces — wondering, *How did Santa know what I did to my brother?*

— were a treat. I also left notes from Santa for our kids while they were young enough to believe.

Birthdays were a joke, too, when our kids were young. We have six birthdays all falling from the end of August to the end of December. The kids would keep asking me who's next, since they thought the parties were just celebrations every few weeks for every member of the family. It took a while before they got the message that it was about the day they were born.

Because it got expensive trying to entertain five kids, I bought a house on Cape Cod, so we could go there for holidays and summer vacations, and it cost less money than renting hotels and airplane flights. It was fun to sit on the beach and watch the fireworks or go whale watching, learn to ride a surfboard, catch fish, and more.

Then there was Halloween, when I dressed up as a monster with various bones from the hospital teaching equipment sticking out of my sleeves and a skull mask. I would go with our kids and other kids so neighbors wouldn't know who I or our kids were. I went to one house where the man had a guard dog to keep people away, and when the dog saw me, he ran and hid; the owner really got a kick out of that. And when I would enter the house, all the dogs and other pets would run and hide under the sofa.

Thanksgiving was always a ritual at my aunt and uncle's house when I was a kid, and now one of our kids does it every year. We all show up to share old stories and laugh about the crazy things they did as kids that their parents are just learning about. It is a rare gift to have everyone together again to relive the past and grow young again. So read on and see how holidays touch our lives.

A Community of Hope

BY BARBARA HOLLACE

The holiday season was approaching, but Fred wasn't feeling very thankful. Sure, he was alive and had a roof over his head, but he was alone. While the television portrayed commercials of loving families gathered around a feast-laden table, Fred only remembered arguments and drunken brawls.

This year might be different; he always hoped that would be the case. It would be different because Fred lived in our apartment building.

My husband and I managed a low-income apartment community in the heart of the city. The non-profit Community Action agency, who owned the property, had a history of helping the most vulnerable in our community since 1966. Our residents were usually people the rest of the world had thrown away. From the mentally ill to those whose lives had once been hostages to their addictions, or military veterans who were looking for a safe place to find peace after a life torn apart by war, our apartment community was a microcosm of today's society. Whether their past was filled with drug and alcohol abuse, broken relationships, or broken promises, we offered them a fresh start. We saw hope in their troubled eyes, when others saw a lost cause.

Thanksgiving has always been one of my favorite holidays, and I was especially determined to make it special this year. Our residents often had little to nothing in their cupboards, so fixing a Thanksgiving feast was out of the question. Several local charities offered free holiday meals if you came to them, but many of our folks were too shy or had medical or mental issues that prevented them from venturing out.

With a little generosity, one stove, and some creative cooking, I developed a plan. Our income was insufficient to feed forty-five people, so to make it happen would take a miracle.

As word spread about my mission, contributions to the meal began to arrive. Our friends and colleagues, who also worked in the same building, enthusiastically asked how they could help. Soon a turkey appeared and the ingredients for side dishes and dessert.

The residents, who would be honored at the dinner, brought what they could spare from their own cupboards or items they had received from the local food bank. They had become an ad hoc family, so their offering, no matter how big or small, was helping a family member to have a good meal. We added our contributions, after scouring the holiday ads for the best deals, and stretching our food budget.

A special invitation was delivered to each resident for a Thanksgiving meal with all the trimmings. They only needed to show up and bring a healthy appetite.

The logistics of cooking two turkeys, dressing, mashed potatoes, pies, and so on, using one stove and one refrigerator, was a miracle in itself. Making the impossible happen was accomplished with the assistance of good-hearted people. Where there was a vacant apartment, the refrigerator was used to store pies and other goodies waiting to be baked. The oven in the office space below was used to heat the stuffing and keep the hot dishes warm until dinner. Residents offered to set up serving tables and arrange chairs in the hallway to create our makeshift dining area.

Residents, both young and old, were seduced from their sacred havens by the smell of turkey as it floated through the hallways. When the food was ready, several people volunteered to help move everything from our apartment to the hallway below, where tables were set up buffet style. As they filed through the line, I saw tears in the eyes of full grown men as they realized that I had done this just for them. Their smiles were payment enough for my labor.

They were not men and women of power and position but former prostitutes, drug addicts, and mentally ill folks. They often appeared in stained and tattered clothing and needing a good bath, but we loved each one of them the same.

I watched Fred come through the line after many had preceded him. He was still cautious, much like an animal sensing there might be a trap waiting to capture him. With Fred, there was no elaborate fanfare. His moves were simple and functional, and his comments often unspoken, yet his body language often told the story.

He took a plate and silverware and surveyed the table that was still heavy laden with the bounty that had been prepared. One spoonful of potatoes was followed by gravy, and the rest of the food that was offered. Slowly, yet meticulously, he made his way to the end and found a seat, with some distance between him and the closest person.

I asked if he wanted a beverage and he politely declined. He began to eat after offering a silent prayer that he inhaled with his next breath. Fred took a few moments to decide where he would start. His stomach was crying out for the food, but you could see his mind struggle with the generosity of the gift his heaping plate represented.

He reached for the homemade biscuit that was tucked on the right-hand side of his plate. I tried not to look and instead surveyed the area and the table to make sure that everyone had what they needed.

I heard a voice behind me. Fred said, "These taste just like the biscuits my grandma made." I struggled to control my tears. "Thank you, Fred," I uttered with my quivering voice. He resumed eating and didn't stop until all his food was gone.

On that Thanksgiving Day, love had turned a ragtag bunch of rejects into a family whose loyalty and commitment rivaled the world's greatest military power.

When the final morsel of food was given away, our residents helped clean up and then returned to their apartments with heads held high. A miracle of love had transformed them into a community of hope.

Frankie's Christmas Miracle

BY JOANNE GENDRON

The day was February 17, 2006. I suddenly had a thought that I needed to get another orange male cat. My orange cat, Max, had passed away the prior year, and my female cat, Willa, needed a friend. I now know why the thought came to me in the middle of a very busy day at work: because it was meant to be.

I searched to find an orange male kitten. My search did not take long; within days I heard from a foster home that they had an orange male. I went to see him, but he had only one eye, and even though I wanted him, the adoption home decided it was better that they not adopt him out. Within days of that, I received another call that there was another orange male kitten that had just arrived; it had been found on the side of the road. I went to see him and had to choose between another orange that had come in. I chose my Frankie.

From the moment we met, it was a love affair. He was quiet and easygoing, even as a kitten. I played with him as often as I could after work, and our bond grew quickly. When Frankie was a year old, it was time to get him and Willa their yearly shots. So off to the vet's we went. My future son-in-law offered to take the cats because the carrier was heavy, and I took my dog, Moe, into the vet's office. As I handed over the carrier, suddenly the cage broke. Willa, my female cat, sat back into the carrier, but Frankie being a young and boisterous man ran into the woods. The vet's office was four miles from my home in the country. My son-in-law ran into the woods to try to get him, but he was nowhere to be found.

I spent the next seven months searching the woods every morning before work and every evening after work. I looked at it as if Frankie thought he was abandoned, so I had to find him and bring him home. I set traps, called him, sent out 750 flyers between two towns, and put up very large posters on telephone poles. The response was remarkable; hundreds of kind people claimed to have seen Frankie, but when I went to see, these cats were not him. I cried every night and tried everything I could to get him back, even telepathy, because our bond was so great.

In the mission to find Frankie, I had traps set up at various locations. I found two skunks, two possums, and two other cats. The skunks were more afraid of me than I was of them, and the possums did not want to get up from their naps in the safe trap. The search for Frankie was an adventure, to say the least.

On the fifth month I decided it was time for me to look for him in a different way; possibly, he might not be alive. And if I did find him not alive, I would bring him home to bury him. I had to get some closure. I also went out and got another orange male kitten, and I named him Freddie.

On December 13, 2007, our dog, Moe, suddenly

got sick. We took him to the vet's, and he was diagnosed with stomach cancer and he passed away.

On Christmas Eve, seven months after we had lost our beloved Frankie, I received a call from a family who had seen an orange male who was very thin and had been attacked by another animal. They managed to coax him into their home and spent the next week and a half getting to know him. They loved him and knew he had come from a loving home. Then they saw the poster and called.

It was a miracle. On Christmas Eve 2007, my prayers were answered. Frankie has been home for over two years now, and I believe that God intervened, sending me two orange cats instead of just one. Frankie and Freddie love each other as if they were natural brothers. I believe that Frankie called to me as a very young kitten to be his human mom because God knew we needed a miracle.

I also believe that Moe, our dog, helped from the other side to send Frankie home. Frankie's homecoming is truly a miracle of love.

Atman/Ananda: A Diwali Miracle

BY RACHEL ASTARTE PICCIONE

November 2003: Fireworks herald my 1 AM arrival at the hotel in Mumbai. Diwali celebrations are underway. This Hindu festival of lights celebrates Atman, our "inner light" that brings forth awareness that all beings are interconnected. For a week, I celebrate by touring Hindu temples, taking in milky incense smoke and sugary pellets doled out by Hindu priests to put sweetness in the mouths of visitors.

On my last day, the Muslim hotel desk clerk suggests I visit Haji Ali mosque. The mosque is a love song to Indo-Islamic architecture. Massive, with intricate clover-top arched entryways. A pure white beacon set far into Worli Bay. According to legend, after the Haji died in Mecca, his coffin miraculously floated to these waters. Before I begin the half-mile-long walk along the causeway, I buy an offering of marigolds wrapped in newspaper.

At the mosque's majestic entrance, my sandals are taken by a boy who squats in dust. He points left. That is where I belong: with the women.

Inside, I hand over my marigold offering, first peeling back its newspaper shroud. My bundle is tossed onto others, identical but for my burst of color, covering the remains of Haji Ali. Behind me, I hear a woman's disapproving *tss.* I turn to see what infraction I've committed. My startled face makes her smile; she waves a dismissive hand.

I sit. Women and children come and go. Through the latticed wooden wall, I watch the men. They are allowed near the shrine, allowed to touch its precious edges.

I consider leaving, but can't, somehow.

Instead, in the heat and flies, I begin to pray. My father, dead nearly two years, comes to me. We'd sat in his cabin and listened to a recording of the Call to Prayer. It reminded him of early mornings in Turkey, where he'd spent a year teaching English. He was dying the night we heard that crimson call. Some peace within us rising.

Now, my head bowed and shrouded, I weep. When this grief passes, it leaves me depleted. Slowly, I gather up simple facts: I am a Jew, praying in a mosque. A woman, sitting among women, relegated to the side, behind metal offering boxes, walled off from our other half, from the holy. What of Diwali's message of Oneness? In an instant, it becomes clear: I pray for peace.

Afterward, I collect my sandals from the crouching boy, adjust my headscarf. Suddenly, I realize the error of my offering. The flowers were to remain wrapped. But I had unveiled them, set the blossoms free one last time.

The following morning as I prepare to leave Mumbai, the daily paper slides, as usual, under my door. The headline reads: "Arafat Calls for Peace Talks." It is a small, huge token. A blossoming toward peace. In Diwali tradition, once the inner light of Atman is achieved, Ananda is realized — the pure light of peace. Now here on my hotel floor, wrapped in newspaper, is an offering of hope.

Santa Magic

BY LEONA SIMON

The April before my sixth birthday, my family moved
to Germany. My father was in the air force and had
been stationed to Ramstien Air Force Base. At some
point after the move I learned about St. Nicholas and
the story of St. Nicholas Eve, which is December 6.
The story is how St. Nick, a Catholic priest, used to
go around Germany just before Christmas to test the
children on their knowledge of catechism. If they
passed the test, they got sweets and goodies; if they
failed, they got switches and pieces of coal. Now it
is celebrated by children leaving their shoes out on
the stoop the night of the fifth to see if St. Nick will
reward them.

I decided that when December 5 arrived I would
do this, but I never told anyone in my family until
the evening of the fifth. Then I got my shoes out and
explained to my family what I was doing and why. As
a young child who had a very strong belief, it didn't
occur to me that no one knew before that night about
what I was expecting, or had any influence on the
possibility of it being created. Further, my mother
was in the hospital recovering from surgery; she had
been a dental hygienist and didn't keep any candy,
gum, or other treats on hand. We were living off-base,
several miles away in a village, and all the stores had

closed for the night. My family had no means of helping to satisfy my desire.

I remember the energy in the air as my family attempted to dissuade me from my plan. My oldest sister explained that maybe St. Nick didn't know a little girl from the States was there, and everyone else chimed in with whatever they could think of to save me from disappointment. Nothing they said changed my mind, and after several minutes of dialogue, my shoes were placed neatly outside the door to wait their fate.

The next morning I got up full of excitement and anticipation. I knew I'd been a good girl and that wonderful things were waiting in my shoes. My family gathered round but stood back a bit, waiting for my reaction and preparing to explain why St. Nick missed me. You could have heard a feather hit the floor as they all held their breath, looking at one another with a "What are we going to tell her?" kind of look.

I swung the door open, and there in the outside hall were my shoes overflowing with chocolate candy coins, hard candies, and nuts. I looked at my family, my heart full of joy, and saw that they were speechless, struck dumb. Again they looked at each other, but now it was with a "Did you do it?" kind of look. They were amazed; none of them had a clue how this had happened.

Later they found out that our landlord, who lived on the floor above us, had seen the empty shoes on his way out to work for the day. He knew that it was

St. Nicholas Day and why the shoes were there, so he promptly returned to his apartment and gathered the goodies he'd leave in the shoes.

My family seemed to forget the miracle of it once they had the "rational" explanation, but I have always known since then that believing, having faith that you deserve to have your desire, that the universe loves you and will respond with miracles when you tune in to it, is the biggest catalyst to receiving what you wish for.

A Jewish Memorial Service for a Romanov on Rosh Hashanah (with Chocolate)

BY STEPHANIE BARBER HAMMER

Ten years ago I had a terrible year. My mother, Barbé Romanovsky-Tirtoff, died, and right afterward my grandmother Stephanya Romanov died, too. I am the only child of only children, and except for my daughter, they were my only living relatives. My mother and I were on bad terms when she died. I had converted to Judaism a few years before, and my mom — a devout atheist and a distant descendent of the Russian royal family — had never forgiven me.

So when my mom died, I felt a double loss: the loss of the person, and the loss of my chance to bridge the chasm of silence that had grown between us. It was particularly painful because I loved and respected my mother. An intellectual, although she never went to college, she taught me about literature, opera, German, and art; she opposed the death penalty and supported abortion rights vigorously and loudly. She had been a very cool mom — until the Jewish thing.

My daughter, Lillian, loved her, too. "When is G. M.'s funeral?" my daughter kept asking. "Can't she have one, even if she wasn't Jewish and didn't believe in God?"

I talked to Rabbi Laura G. about the situation.

"What did your mother love?" Laura asked.

I replied, without thinking, "Chocolate."

"Then have a chocolate memorial buffet for her," Laura said. "And, since she wasn't religious, pick a writer she liked and use that writer for readings."

Without hesitation, I chose Wendy Wasserstein. My mother loved her writing because Wasserstein loved eating and men. Barbé Romanovsky-Tirtoff liked boys. She watched sports so she could admire the fit and the fabulous.

We scheduled the memorial service at my house shortly before Rosh Hashanah, the Jewish New Year. We took turns reading from Wendy Wasserstein's hysterical essay collection *Bachelor Girls*, and after Laura led us in Kaddish, we circulated around the hot fudge, the flourless chocolate cake, and the brownies.

The days leading up to Rosh Hashanah are important. You have the chance to regret your mistakes and ask the people you've wronged for forgiveness. You get to forgive others as well. And you get to forgive yourself for not being perfect, for getting angry, and for not knowing how to make things right.

At the memorial chocolate buffet, I forgave my mother for being angry about Judaism, and I asked — over my plate of brownies — to be forgiven for the hurt I caused her.

That night, I dreamed my mother called me on the telephone. We talked for a moment and suddenly I remembered.

"Mom — you're dead," I told her, and she replied

in her warm low voice, "Do you really think that matters?"

It doesn't. It also doesn't matter what you believe, and whether you're a Russian Princess or a Jewish American Princess, as long as there is love and forgiveness.

And chocolate.

Miracle Memo

I think what we all learn from these stories is what the age-old message tells us: that faith, hope, love, and chocolate are what make the world go 'round, and that is clearly seen at holiday time. We are all here to play the part of being God's body, and so when we act the way Barbara Hollace did, we are bringing God down to earth for these people, and once they feel that God loves them, a miracle truly is brought into being. We are all capable of doing this, but you must feel self-love and self-worth and know that God loves you in order to share the love with others. We are all made from the same stuff God is made of and we are all family.

Someday I pray we will all become one family, and then truly the greatest of miracles will occur, since we will have created a world that will be perfect because of the love everyone shares. The Garden of Eden will be here with us. With it will come Ananda and bliss. We need to understand the message of religions and not get lost in words and rituals, which cause problems and make God unhappy. Look at Barbara's love-filled Thanksgiving; what a miracle in action that was.

What I have learned from my animal-intuitive friend Amelia Kinkade is that when you worry and grieve, your intellect gets in the way and you cannot connect with the missing animal's consciousness. Searching, grieving, worrying, nothing happens. When Joanne Gendron finds closure and peace, then adopts another cat, look what happens. Joanne gets a phone call because Frankie knows he needs to get in touch with Joanne. It was why the still pond and water play an important role in myths and religions. Only when our life and mind are still can we see our true self in the reflection and know where our lost animal is.

The day I adopted our dog Buddy, I stopped on the way home for gas. As I opened the door, Buddy jumped out of the car and ran into the street. Everyone was stopping their cars and trying to help me. We finally caught him and I drove home. When we arrived, I calmly approached Buddy in the back of my SUV and formed words in my mind asking him why he acted as he did. I could hear him telling me that he had belonged to a couple. The husband was an alcoholic who abused him and locked him in the car when he went out drinking instead of taking him for a walk. I told him I would never treat him that way. It has taken him a long time to not back away when I pick up a stick of any sort, from a broom to a broken branch.

A few weeks later I drove to the supermarket with Buddy and Furphy in our minivan. When I came out of the market, I saw the side door on the minivan was wide open. I realized I must have hit the car key control as I was putting the keys in my pocket. I was sure Buddy would be gone, but when I arrived at the car, he was calmly sitting there. Furphy was gone. So I started yelling his name, until I heard Amelia saying, "Bernie, calm down and get in the animal's head." I did and immediately knew he was in the supermarket looking for me. So off I went, and sure enough the security guard saw me coming and asked, "Is this your dog?" He had given him treats and cared for him.

I have also left Furphy at the rear door of a cafeteria because they did not allow animals, knowing he would be there waiting for me — only to have someone come walking through the cafeteria carrying him and asking, "Whose dog is this?" Furphy is a wise guy and found his way around to and in the front door. So they gave him permission to stay under our table, impressed by his determination to be with me.

Rachel Piccione is correct: we should not keep separating ourselves from one another because of our races, religions, and more. We are one family and need to accept that, if we are to survive and preserve the home we all share: planet earth. We are all sheep, and even though the color of our wool varies, we are all the same color inside. Differences are for recognition and not a reason for separation.

Leona Simon was a child who didn't give up or listen to her family try to discourage her. She lived the message that was within her, and the universe responded by providing her with what she asked for and needed.

Over God's desk there are two plaques, which tell us about how to live our lives, and religion is not the issue or the message. The first plaque says, "Don't feel personally, totally, eternally, irrevocably responsible for everything; that's my job." The second one fits what Stephanie Hammer did with her relationship with her mom. It says, "Everything you remember I forget, and everything you forget I remember. When we take responsibility and let love and forgiveness in, we do not deny anything but we do heal all the lives involved." This last message comes from the teachings of the Jewish High Holidays.

Indeed, life isn't about what we believe; it is about how we act. If we imitated God instead of letting words become our God, then the world would be a very tolerant place. Life is a miracle. Creation is a miracle. There has to be an intelligent, loving, conscious energy behind it all. What we call it and how we worship is not the issue. We simply need to accept that science and religion are really one when our minds remain open to possibilities.

As Stephanie's mom related, being dead doesn't mean you are not conscious. As Stephanie says, it doesn't matter what you believe, but what you experience. So do not let words and beliefs become your God, and so close your mind and limit yourself. Open your mind and observe the miracle of life.

When you send out holiday greetings this year, remember to include the wish for peace of mind.

CHAPTER THIRTEEN

Endings Are Never the End

Every new beginning comes from some other beginning's end.

— *Seneca*

The caterpillar melts away and transforms into the butterfly, the symbol of transformation, and then struggles to be free of the cocoon and begin a new life. That is what we are all here to accomplish and do: to see our life as an endless series of beginnings and to constantly be born again to a new life. As Joseph Campbell said, only birth can overcome death — not the rebirth of something old but the birth of something new. That is what I try to teach people so they can heal by creating a new life.

There's something especially heartbreaking about the passing of children and animals. They share an innocence, and often upon their passing, we feel a sense of injustice in our assumption that they didn't have long enough on this earth. Yet, through so many of these experiences, these loved ones teach us what it is to truly live.

I once had a four-year-old patient named Amber; her mother, Patti DiMiceli, tells her story in this chapter. Amber is with me all the time because whenever I lecture I show a slide of her drawing. Amber has been a teacher for many thousands of people and is immortal through her love. Many years ago, I walked into Amber's hospital room and looked at the drawing she had done that day. It revealed a purple balloon, with a line of black draped over it, going up out of the picture. I knew it meant she was ready to leave her body and make the spiritual transition, which the color purple can symbolize. Several things in the drawing puzzled me, however.

At the bottom of the page was the face, in yellow and green, of a child crying. Those are healthy colors and didn't fit her desire to die. I asked Amber about it, and she said, "Oh that's not me; that's the child in the next room crying." Then there was a line made up of many balls of color, like decorations, ending at a cup with a four-pointed star in it. I couldn't interpret what that meant. However, I told Patti that it was time to stop focusing on cancer treatment and to take Amber home and love her. I explained what I knew from the drawing and what I couldn't interpret. Patti took Amber home, where she died peacefully on Patti's birthday. When I later counted the colored dots, they turned out to be the days left in Amber's life.

The yard around our home is a graveyard for all our beloved pets. Each has a gravesite, and they remain teachers for me. Each animal taught me something about my behavior and what I need to incorporate into my life to be a better person.

After one of our dogs died, I began to build a cairn of stones at his gravesite. Every morning I would look for a stone to add to the structure. One morning I heard him say to me, "Why don't you bring me a flower?" That changed my attitude for the entire day because now I was looking for beauty and not a stone.

Animals are indeed teachers and healers. Our bonding hormones rise when we pet a furry creature, and survival statistics for many illnesses are better when there are furry animals in the house. Not to mention that many women meet the man they will marry walking their dog.

If we raised our children the way we train and raise our beloved pets — with love, trust, respect, consistency, exercise, affection, and discipline — this would be a healthier and more peaceful world.

Although the following stories each have an ending, the people who tell them were able to see them as only another beginning in their lives.

The Miracle of Change

BY PATTI DiMICELI

As a child, I knew I was chosen. Decades would pass until I would learn why.

The summer of 1979 was hot, humid, and full of hope. As a single mother, I worked construction to support my four-year-old daughter, Amber, and myself. It was strenuous and challenging, but the pay was good and my life was finally looking up — until I looked down and saw the lump behind Amber's right ear. "Oh my God! *Cancer!*" I silently screamed, then heard a voice. "It's not you; it's Amber." The premonition I had at her birth — that I would die before she was six — was wrong.

Several months passed as I searched for a doctor who would look further. By the time they did, the diagnosis was bleak: "Rhabdomyosarcoma, third stage." The media spread our story around the world as we searched for *all* cancer therapies, not just chemotherapy and radiation. We chose an immunotherapy researching center in Freeport, Bahamas.

Amber responded to the immunotherapy, but after that she came down with tonsillitis, and then a new tumor grew. Having left the United States, we couldn't find a surgeon to help us "debulk" the growing tumor. Dr. Burton sent us to the Children's Hospital in Montreal, to see if Canadian surgeons could help.

Test after test was performed. In the end, the

Canadians could not help her either. We left the hospital and set off to fulfill Amber's dreams. "Mom, I want to be a ballerina," she said with childlike joy. We found a dance shop in Old Montreal and left with a complete outfit: tutu, tights, ballet slippers, and real toe shoes.

Settling into our hotel room, I gave Amber a bath and tucked her into bed. I went into the bathroom to take the longest shower of my life. The hot water went on forever and my thoughts began to flow: "Cancer… the tumor… my little girl… my baby. How can I bear this, God? I am so human… so weak. *Are you here? Are you listening???*"

I sat on the floor and put my head on my knees, then I heard: "I'm here. Don't look ahead. Take each decision as it is presented, no sooner. You will be my arrow, but I will point the way."

"Okay, God, *show me! I need to see you to know you exist!*" I lay down on the floor and cried until I couldn't anymore.

I emerged from the bathroom and saw my miracle sleeping. I stood there transfixed. Amber lay on her back like an angel with her tutu on, her toe shoes poking up through the blankets, and her arms around her ballerina slipper bag. My eyes looked for her wings, but only my soul could see them. "Embrace the angel. Love her completely. Don't ever leave her. Don't ever let her go."

We returned to the United States and desperately searched for a surgeon to help us… to help Amber *live*. I found Dr. Bernie Siegel. From the moment he walked into the room, I knew he was different. He shook Amber's hand and began talking with *her*, not me. He agreed to admit her to St. Raphael's to see if he could operate. "What about the publicity, the controversy?" I asked, knowing Amber's journey through cancer had been followed by the media from the start. After exhausting the traditional treatments, I'd decided to go outside of the "medical establishment" for alternative therapies. It was a decision that was not only highly controversial but might prompt the traditional doctors to file legal action to call me "unfit," take Amber away from me, and force her to undergo the cancer treatments they saw fit.

"I don't *have* to be a doctor," he said with such confidence that I instantly felt thankful and willing to give up control. "I'll treat her as my own," he assured me.

At that moment, nothing mattered more to Bernie than doing what he could to save Amber — not other doctors, or what treating her might do to his reputation, or the controversy swirling around the issue of alternative cancer treatment.

While Amber was undergoing tests, I went to the hospital gift shop. As I stood in line, I heard a voice. "Turn around." I spotted a large, shiny brass key. "Give this to Amber. It is the Key to Heaven. Tell her she won't have to knock. She can open the Golden Gates herself." I knew it was time to let her go.

Bernie began to teach us how to help her cross over, to make the transition between life and death, between this world and the one beyond. Using "Spontaneous Drawings," he encouraged Amber to draw, and interpreted their meaning for us. She was ready, and now I was, too.

With Bernie's support and a supply of morphine, I left the hospital and brought Amber home to die. The next few weeks I kept the tape recorder on. I didn't want to miss a word of her wisdom. She was sent to teach me and to teach all of us about life and about death. "Mom, I know I'm here to help a lot of people," she said. And the wisdom kept coming.

One day, she called me to her side and gave me the gift that changed my life forever. "Mom, when I die, I'll still be Amber, I'll just be *different.*" I now know that we do not "pass away" and that I haven't "lost a child." Death is simply *change.*

At 12:05 AM, on my twenty-seventh birthday, Amber slipped into a coma. I dressed her in the outfit she picked to "die and go to Heaven," laid her on the sofa, and stayed at her side. Her breathing was labored. She sounded tired, weary of the pain and ready to be free.

A tear fell from her eye. And then another. And another. "Amber, it's okay. Don't cry. I'll be all right. I promise. I love you." She could hear me. "Go, now, Amber. Be with God. Be with God, Amber." As I finished these words, she stopped breathing. Her face lit up and glowed like an angel. My body began to tingle from head to toe as I *physically felt God!* The only words I could utter slipped out: "Thank you, God. Thank you."

Amber's death was my miracle. She didn't leave me; she changed. I see her in the dance of a leaf as it

falls to the ground, the butterflies that visit my butterfly garden, Annie's (our Jack Russell terrier's) humorous antics, the things that she left behind. My heart
is not broken — it is open to the possibility of seeing
her and the many small ways she still says, "Hi, Mom!
I'm here!"

Reopening to Love

BY JEANETTE LeBLANC

In one of his more recent books, 101 Exercises for the Soul, Bernie says, "The ideal role model comes with a fur coat." I have to agree.

At a Colorado animal shelter, after I inquired about the "poodle in sick bay," a tiny quaking pixie of a dog was first handed to me. He seemed to melt into the curve of my arm — his shaking stopped and his soulful black oval eyes silently spoke, "Please love me."

No one else did, or at least no one came for him. So a week later I showed up to claim him as my own, naming him Pierre.

My husband and son loved him dearly, but he was clearly my dog — claiming my lap the moment I sat down. His spontaneous aerial flips of joy each and every time I walked in the front door felt like a canine standing ovation. "Momma's home!"

Soon well-loved, fed, and nurtured, his apricot fur grew silky and his slender frame filled out as he became an aficionado of universal dog thrills — adventure walks, spontaneous car rides, and tasty treats. He loved to luxuriate in the sun — sometimes belly up with a slight smile, an irrefutable grin on his slender poodle face.

Time rushed by like a surreal Sunday drive in the family car — so many memories of sight, sound, and scent. Pierre's diamond-shaped dog nose sniffed away along every ride as we moved from bluff-side suburbs to the desert to an island in the Pacific Northwest.

Over a decade passed and my son grew up from a rambunctious preschooler to a high schooler, while my husband and I had unexpectedly crossed over into our forties, officially "middle-aged." Pierre was still spry — yet a senior dog — with an enlarged heart and failing vision. He napped more and played less, but still loved to bark at the deer that would wander up the backyard hill and elude the eagles overhead on our seaside beach walks. I kept him close and soon was carrying him up and down stairs and spending every minute I could with him. The vet reassured me that I was doing all that I could and that "if I were a dog, I'd want to be your dog." Strange comfort, indeed.

Instead of walks, we started going for long sun naps in the backyard. I gently placed him on the freshly cut lawn — grass under his paws, the breeze caressing his thinning fur, nose sniffing. That poodle smile was back — lips curled ever so gently up. His eyes had grown opaque — cataracts had recently turned his brown-black eyes a ghostly shade of blue. He looked at me, almost through me. *Please don't go*, I thought. I lay down on the grass next to him to share the sun's warmth and feel the pulsing of his heartbeat just a little while longer.

This would be the spot where we would bury him, wrapped in a silken red blanket, with flowers and whispered prayers as if it would stop the cold dampness of the earth or the quaking sobs that would soon come when I was home alone. I let the grass grow up and cover his grave, preferring my memories inside. It was still too painful.

People told me to get another dog. I don't think so, I said. Then, in a weak moment, charmed by animal calendar–worthy cuteness, two poodle puppies came home with me.

Zoey is stuffed-animal cute — a ball of white fluff with a black button nose, one apricot-shaded ear, and a way of tilting her head from side to side when she's intensely curious. Chloe is a real dog — classic toy-poodle looks, slightly off-white, brown nose. She's territorial and bossy to her sister, though Zoey weighs an entire pound more. They're adorable. I'm depressed.

I throw them their toys. I housebreak them — they're smart, so it doesn't take long. Every day I take care of them; I pet them, feed them, and play with them. Chloe and Zoey are not Pierre. They never will be. Pierre was a dog like no other — one who captured my eternal devotion with his beyond-human personality, resilient grace, and heroic will-to-live, not unlike Bernie's extraordinary pet rabbit Smudge. How could two sweet but goofy little sister pups ever compare?

One day I call for them, they don't come. They always come, all wiggles and tails a-wagging. Yet they are not anywhere. I search upstairs and down, in every room. I rush out and call their names — nothing. I go out back, heart pounding, fearful of an open gate.

When I see them, they are lying side by side like twin sentries in the exact spot where we buried Pierre. Oddly calm, not playing, not napping, but sitting hyper-aware, as if curious about something unseen. Zoey tilts her head.

I drop to a sitting position on the grass and tears start to fall.

They see me now. I bear witness to two sets of eyes — two unique dogs — both clearly expressing, "Please love me." Like Pierre, but not him. They watch me with growing puppy anticipation. I want to. I really do. To do that once again, I'll have to breathe, to grieve, and to let go. I take that deep breath. There is enough love. I feel my own answer: I will and I do. I smile, and Zoey and Chloe come running.

Asking the Ancestors to Appear

BY KAYLA FINLAY

One of the most memorable years for my family was 2007. My adoptive dad had died in February of a fast-growing brain tumor; I then moved my mother, who had Alzheimer's, down to Virginia to be near my brother. Then on July 5, my soon-to-be husband and his best friend, Carl, were riding their motorcycles when Carl suddenly drove into the rear of a car and was killed instantly. The moments that followed were a blur. For days all of us were in shock. My fiancé and I had known each other for twenty years, but we had hesitated on formally committing to marriage. However, when death struck so close, our way of looking at life shifted, and perhaps with more appreciation, in the emotions of the moment, he and I decided to finally get married.

The events that followed in the next two weeks were exceptionally amazing. My fiancé asked his best friend's widow to be the "best person" to stand in at the ceremony in place of her now-deceased husband. Wishing my dad could be there, I asked his best friend's father to do me the honor of walking me down the aisle.

Our "best person" was graciously, if temporarily, being pulled from her widowed grief by the thought of something good coming from all this tragedy. She always thought we should be married, and she jumped into planning this wedding ceremony with a joy and love for life even amidst her own pain and loss.

It was intended to be a small private ceremony but grew into a full-blown wedding ceremony, complete with white gown, maid of honor, and a healing center that was filled with our family and friends. We chose a combination traditional and alternative-style ceremony and an interfaith minister to perform the honors, with drumming and smudging in honor of my Native American heritage.

During the introduction to the ceremony, we invited the spirits of our ancestors to join us in celebration of the day, and then we specifically invited the spirits of my father and of my husband's best friend, Carl. There was a feeling of beauty and love in the air that day. Two weeks after the death of a dear friend, we all found ourselves celebrating life and love. The feeling was a magical and almost mystical one, and all the guests commented on that for a long time afterward.

To include our guests in the celebration process, we left a basket of throwaway cameras for them to use in order to capture their views of this special day. At the end, we asked them to put the cameras back in the basket, and we would have the photos developed. Little did we think that someone would capture a photograph of my dad's spirit rising from the room adjacent to where the ceremony was held — a room in which he lived surrounded by our family for the six months prior to his death. When we first viewed the photo, it took my breath away. I had never seen anything like it! There were three orbs of energy that originated from the window of his room, went up to the sky, and then returned back to the window.

I showed the photo to our "best person" and then to Carl's parents. His mother said something quite unexpected. She looked at it and quite simply said, "Oh, how nice someone got a photo of that. I saw that myself." When I asked why on earth she didn't point it out to the rest of us when she first saw it, she said, "Well, I saw it and just said that someone was watching out over you, and the person who was standing behind me agreed."

I had the photo enlarged in the hopes that it would either reveal more detail or that the image would dissipate. The more it was enlarged, the more we knew what we were seeing. When I showed it to the professional photographer who had been our guest at the ceremony, he paled and said, "It's just what you think it is. It's not a spot on the negative or an illusion. It's giving me chills just looking at it."

Each person who saw it had a similar reaction of disbelief and goose bumps.

A few months passed, and I received a call from a friend who was also at the wedding. She told me that she finally got her film developed from her own camera, and she had a photo that had an unusual image in it. I immediately said, "Oh, the photo of the wedding party on the front lawn with the trailing orbs of Dad's spirit coming out of the window?"

Was I surprised when she said, "No, this is a photo of your 'best person' inside the gallery as she was walking back down the aisle, after the ceremony. You have to see this. There is this ball of light zipping around her." I knew it was Carl. We had invited the spirits of Dad and Carl, and they accepted the invitation to our wedding at Spirit Creek.

Miracle Memo

As Patti DiMiceli described, she took Amber home. On her mother's birthday, Amber died. Later, Patti told me over the phone that Amber had come to her that day and said, "Mom, I'm dying today as a gift to you to free you from all the trouble." When I went and looked at Amber's drawing and counted the colorful spots, I realized they represented the number of days left in Amber's life and that the four-pointed star was her birthday present and decoration representing her life and rebirth and Patti's birthday, too.

Patti's closing words about butterflies, leaves, and pets are also quite fitting. The butterfly is the symbol of transformation, and the fall leaves tell us to reveal our beauty before we let go of the tree of life. Life is truly a series of beginnings. When we use every experience as a teacher, we start a new life with the lessons we learned, rather than end our lives because we are fearful of change.

Jeanette LeBlanc's dogs, Chloe and Zoey, became her therapists because they knew what she was thinking and feeling. So can all animals, if we but listen and watch for what they are trying to tell us.

Jeanette mentions Smudge, our house bunny, who was a teacher, too. She would jump up on the sofa and take whatever I was reading in her teeth, throw it on the floor, and say to me, "Rub my tummy." But what really helped convince me about animal communication was our evening routine: in the morning she would run out through the pet door, but every evening I would have to go out to bring her in from our fenced-in yard. She would run all around avoiding me. So one night I said, consciously but nonverbally, "Why don't you let me pick you up and bring you into the house?" Her answer, which I could hear in my head: "You don't treat the cats that way." I went on to explain that I was worried about her and possible predators and that the cats could protect themselves. From that night on, she let me pick her up without trying to avoid me.

It is easy for me to read and accept what Kayla Finlay experienced because, in my personal and professional life, I have experienced very similar mystical events. I would ask all who read this to be willing to accept and believe in their experience and not close their minds to things they can't understand or explain. On a personal level, when my dad died, those in the room saw him leave his body in a way similar to what Kayla describes in her photos.

I think her wedding created fertile soil for an event like this to occur. Everyone was in a place of peace and love and healing the wounds of their loss, and, therefore, open to the presence of the mystical and spiritual elements, which surround us at all times.

I can't help but add that it is also our pets that help us to laugh every day. Our cat Miracle lived for over twenty years and was a gift and a miracle, and she chose to die on one of our son's birthdays so she would never be forgotten.

I think this wonderful quote below says it all:

Our life is an apprenticeship to the truth
that around every circle another can be drawn;
that there is no end in nature,
but every end is a beginning, and under
every deep a lower deep opens.
— *Ralph Waldo Emerson*

CHAPTER FOURTEEN

Miracles from Beyond

Perhaps they are not stars, but rather openings in heaven where the love of our lost ones pours through and shines down upon us to let us know they are happy.

— *Eskimo proverb*

My father and his brother cared for the family's burial site. As a child I often went with them to help while they tidied up and cared for the plants and headstones. What I thought was sick was their lying on the ground at the sites they would one day be buried in and discussing which way they wanted to lie relative to the view and sunshine.

Well, when my dad died, and his coffin was brought to his gravesite, it was in the opposite direction to what he had wanted. I felt bad as they lifted his coffin, and then the men doing it turned the coffin completely around, reversing the position of his head and feet, and lowered it into the grave. There was no way I could explain how the men got the message and did what they did, but my dad's wish came true.

There are signs that communication can occur through consciousness and does not require a body. When my folks died, I received a call from a mystic friend, Monica; she did not live near us and so did not consciously know anything about my family. Monica told me my folks were together and very happy and being shown around by someone who liked chocolate and cigarettes. "Do you know who that is?" Before I could answer, she said, "Oh, it's Elisabeth Kübler-Ross. She's showing your folks around." Yes, Elisabeth was a dear friend and teacher of mine.

Years ago, I had injured my leg training for a road race. While attending a holistic medical meeting, my wife and I met Olga Worrall. Olga was a world-famous healer. She had once been tested by atomic physicists and others and demonstrated how her hands could change the course of atomic particles and energize water; plants grew faster when watered by her treated water than plants watered with untreated water. My wife told me to go and ask her to heal me. I was a nonbeliever and too embarrassed to ask. So my wife went ahead and asked her.

Olga came over to where I was sitting and put her two hands on my thigh. I felt like two hot irons were placed there. When I put my hands on my leg, I felt no heat at all. After several minutes, Olga stopped and I stood up completely free of pain and had no trouble jogging the next day. Olga's comment was that she was not the healer. She was simply the conduit for the energy of the universe and directed it through her hands. I have learned we are all potential conduits for this universal energy.

I had to agree with her after that experience.

In the following stories, Rowena, Andrea, and Cindy all experienced communication with loved ones who had passed — a feat that is nothing short of a miracle.

A Sense of Humor

BY ROWENA WILLIAMSON

My husband, Phil, and I often said that our marriage was based on love and a sense of humor. He loved harmless practical jokes. I loved giving him goofy presents. Once for his birthday, I gave him a life-size cardboard cutout of his favorite movie star, John Wayne, which took up residence in his workshop, where he built beautiful furniture.

Opening my closet door one day, I reached in for something and realized a man was standing in the shadows. I screamed and jumped backward. Then I heard a telltale giggle from the TV room. Yep, Pilgrim, ol' John had been put in among my clothes.

When Phil was diagnosed with incurable cancer, he dealt with the pain quietly, but with flashes of his old humor, madly ringing a call bell just to bring me into the bedroom so he could grin at me. Eventually, Phil died, and I lost the love of my life. That night, after a day of grief so deep I could hardly breathe, I fell asleep sometime after 2 AM. It seemed only minutes later that the bed lamp, which was bolted into the wall, fell right next to my pillow. I got out of bed and turned on the overhead light. I felt oddly calm as I looked around our bedroom.

"Phil?" I asked. Was this a last example of his unquenchable humor? I know I felt him near me.

Ring of Love

BY ANDREA HURST

It was a difficult year. I had lost my best friend to cancer, my marriage was dissolving, and now here I was doing a last walk-through before moving out of the family home. I longed for my grandmother's loving support and the strength she always displayed to me. But she had passed years ago, and the one possession I still had that had been hers, a small platinum and gold ring, was missing, too.

I had hoped I would find the delicate ring when I packed, but that was not the case. I walked through my kids' bedrooms, now so very empty, and then out the back door into the yard. The new buyers had been clear: they wanted the mini-barn completely empty as well. What possibly was still left in there? My husband told me he had cleaned out all his tools and boxes.

I entered the barn and scanned the walls. A few garden supplies remained, and I gathered them to take with me. On a shelf in the very back was a twelve-foot plastic vacuum hose that belonged to a machine we had not owned in years. I sighed. Why in the world had Michael left this for me to dispose of?

I tried to lift it off the shelf, but it was so bulky and heavy I had to heave it up and onto my shoulders. Just as the plastic landed on my collarbone, I heard a soft whish of air and the sound of something dropping to the wood floor. I couldn't believe what I saw: my grandmother's ring sparkled at my feet.

What were the chances that the one item left behind would hit my shoulder just right? I knew it was my grandmother, reaching across from the other side, filling me with the miracle of her love, and being right there with me every step of the way.

Love Never Dies

BY CINDY HURN

Separated by two countries and an ocean, Dad and I had
not seen each other for several years, and he was quite
ill. In 2001, I returned to the States to begin a new life.
At first I flew to the East Coast, staying with my sister and brother, but before leaving for the West Coast,
I went to visit Mom and Dad in Florida. During the
afternoon, my stepmother went to the hairdresser's so
that Dad and I could have some time alone together;
she knew it would probably be our last visit.

"Dad, when you die, how will I know you're still
there?" I asked.

Without batting an eyelash, he replied, "Love
never dies. Our hearts will always be together. But,
if you miss me, look up to the sky. When you see an
eagle, you'll know I'm with you."

Knowing my father's affinity with birds, particularly with bald eagles, I wasn't surprised at his answer.
Years before, when he visited my house in Canada, he
was fascinated with two eagles that nested high in the
Douglas fir behind our secluded property. Each time
he stood outside, it seemed as if they knew him; they
circled high above him and called down in spearing
cries until he smiled and acknowledged them.

When I settled in Sacramento, I kept an eye on
the skies. Although I often saw buzzard hawks, ravens,
and other birds of prey, I never saw any eagles. The

area was too populated. How, I wondered, would Dad's spirit reach me, if there weren't any eagles here? After he died, I kept hoping I'd see some sign of him, but no eagle circled; no eagle cried.

Three months later, a package arrived. Sent directly from a catalog company, it contained a packing slip with my stepmother's return address on it. What could it be? Mom never sent presents. I called her, thinking she might have made a mistake. "I don't know what came over me," she laughed apologetically. "I just saw this kite catalog the other day, and suddenly I had an overwhelming urge to order one for you. So I did! I hope you enjoy flying it. Let me know how it goes."

Still puzzled, I opened the package, and following instructions, began to assemble the kite. First, I put bamboo struts into wide-stretched wings and a tail. Next, I attached them to the back of a bird-shaped body, as shown in the diagram. I then flipped the body over and pulled the string until the bird's head, with its strong hooked beak, rose into position. When the final string was pulled, the chest expanded, exposing a bright red heart painted across the breast. I looked into the bird's piercing eyes that stared straight into mine, and its open prey mouth crying without a sound. Suddenly I realized — it was my eagle!

I called Mom back and asked her what prompted the gift. Had Dad ever told her what we discussed? "No," she said, perplexed at my question. "When I saw the kite, I just thought of you, and I had to get it, that's all. Is there something wrong?"

"Not a thing, Mom. You couldn't have done better."

No matter where I live now, whether in a city, town, or countryside, when I sit down at my desk to write, I have the comforting awareness that, hanging from the ceiling and looking over my shoulder, there is an eagle with widespread wings and a bright red heart painted across its breast.

Miracle Memo

There is a wisdom, awareness, and knowledge within all of us that communicates with the collective unconscious when we are in need. Andrea Hurst needed a sign, and her grandmother's ring miraculously appeared. She was given the gift she needed right at that moment.

Rowena Williamson's marriage sounds a lot like mine. I created a new word, *liove*. It means to live and love and laugh, too. That's what relationships are made of. I put away all the groceries my wife brought home one day, and all she did was criticize me for putting tomatoes in the fridge. So I wrote her a poem called "Divorce." She laughed and we fired the divorce lawyer and took the tomatoes out of the fridge. Laughter eliminates fear and heals our pain.

The lamp falling is no coincidence. When people feel safe, they share mystical events that have happened to them. We can hear our loved ones' voices, see their spirits, or find things that had meaning to them. After his son died, one Connecticut man had a beautiful butterfly accompany him as he went for a walk. His son had collected butterflies, and when the man returned home, he looked up the butterfly in his son's books and found it only lived in South America.

I was running a support group for cancer patients, and one woman was talking about her daughter, who had died and loved birds. She was describing how a loud bird had interrupted her sister's outdoor wedding, and everyone felt it was her daughter. At that moment a bird flew in the window of our room, and of course everyone felt her daughter was appearing again. I may add that, in the many years I sat in that room, never had a bird even come close to the window.

Love is permanent, as Cindy's title states, and so it is always present and ready to be felt and known by those who are living in the moment. Sooner or later all our bodies will perish, so if you want to be immortal, love someone. Love is the only thing of permanence, and the bridge between the world of the living and the world of the dead.

Believe, and the door will be opened
for your miracles, too.

CHAPTER FIFTEEN

Bernie as a Miracle

Bernie Siegel...My Miracle

*I knew Bernie more than thirty years ago — long
before the world did. He had not written any book yet.*

*He had a compassion that was more than most.
He would sit in a room with a dying patient for hours
so that person would know that someone cared.*

*He would stand in a hospital alone fighting for his
convictions and insights that were far beyond that of
the average doctor. After many struggles he won.*

*He was never afraid of the dying patient. He gave them
the courage to live.*

*He showed them that they did have an identity worth
fighting for.
He was — and is — a miracle.*

— Susan Duffy

When people say *I* inspire them, I know it is because the inspiration I am bringing out resides within them. I cannot put it there. I know I am the coach, and they are the real stars and performers, but I also know we can be a team. Nature gives us the opportunity to create miracles. When I decided to travel less, but still wanted to continue to help people, I asked nature what to do. Nature responded by showing me how plants spread seeds while they remain in the same place. So I decided to spread my seeds, and through books, emails, lectures, and more, I can be found all over the world.

To Write Again

BY JENNIFER GIUFFRE-DONOHUE

I was required to read one of Bernie Siegel's books in college and was hooked on his positivity from that moment on. The stories of his unconventional ideas and the exceptional patients he wrote about were so amazing to me and had such a big impact on how I saw life from then on. Who knew that so many years later I would look to Dr. Bernie and his CDs again to get through my own cancer experience?

I'm an aspiring writer, and when I started going through chemo, even though I'm a very positive person, I lost my drive to write. I was just too tired and not in the mood. One day, while waiting to go in for treatment, I had one of Dr. Bernie's books in my hand. Another patient noticed what I was reading and struck up a conversation with me because he had one of his books with him as well. It turned out that among other things, he was an eighty-year-old writer. He was actually a published author, and he was currently working on a new book.

We would see each other at various times and became friends. Sometimes he wore a duck hat, and I would think to myself, he's definitely a fan of Dr. Bernie. He really put a smile on my face. He unfortunately passed away due to his cancer, but he left a lasting impression on me and gave me the inspiration to pick up my pen again. I thought to myself, "If he can do it, then so can I."

"Indoctoration"

BY DR. MATT MUMBER

A miracle can be defined as the sudden awareness of
letting go of an old way of seeing or being. In this
sense, Bernie has orchestrated several miracles on my
journey to becoming a radiation oncologist — a doctor who treats cancer patients with radiation therapy.

My initiation into being a doctor — what I like
to call "indoctoration" — was summarized by one of
our clinical attending physicians during the first year
of medical school. It was a beautiful sunny day in the
spring, and directly after a brief lunch break, the class
was having a more difficult time than usual settling
into the semidarkened auditorium-style classroom.
This attending physician and teacher was different
than the litany of basic science PhDs who had been
instructing us about the minutia of biochemical,
histologic, and physiologic functions in the human
body. This teacher was an actual human doctor — a
practicing physician here to start our Introduction
to Clinical Medicine course — a much-awaited foray
into what we were all there for: being with patients.
He was cloaked in the traditional clinical medicine
uniform — a long, bright white lab coat extending
to near his knees, his name and clinical department
embroidered on the pocket, and stethoscope tucked
in a large side pocket, partially protruding out. The
combination of spring air and excitement over this

leap into patient-focused care created a palpable buzz in the normally stale room.

After a few minutes of hustling and bustling among the students, one of my classmates had the audacity to ask, "Can we have our class outdoors in order to enjoy the day?"

The attending half-smiled and wearily replied, "You all have got to get settled. You'll learn not to look outside." With audible groans, the class quickly transitioned back into information reception mode.

This statement — "You'll learn not to look outside" — defines the attitude with which we were encouraged to learn how to serve ourselves and our fellow human beings as doctors. We were taught to look only to our academic textbooks and the scientific literature, and to avoid looking at more fuzzy things like our own personal physical, emotional, or spiritual needs. This quickly translated into seeing patients as operational organisms constituting all the various functions that we had been memorizing for tests. The patient's unique emotional, physical, and spiritual characteristics were important only to the extent that they could be measured and clearly defined. Our job was to identify and battle disease as it presented in human organisms in a measurable way.

I had thought of leaving medicine before I read Bernie's *Love, Medicine & Miracles* in the summer after my first year of medical school. I met him on the lecture circuit that summer, and I saw for myself that looking outside of the books and into the person was not only effective medicine but was what being a doctor was all about. Bernie reminded me of what I knew in my heart — of what called me to medicine — the service of self and others with love. This love made sense. It helped to relieve suffering and encourage the enjoyment of life. It also worked — it made the human organism healthy in ways that mere biomechanical processes could not.

Bernie encouraged me to look all around, internally and externally, in as many ways as possible. When it was time to pick a specialty, he helped me to make that selection through the use of picture drawing, a miraculous tool for healing and awareness. Now twenty years later, I am amazed by the near-clairvoyant accuracy of the picture that led me to choose radiation oncology. It is a montage that clearly predicted much of what my daily life contains today, in sometimes specific detail: three children, working with a retreat center, holding hands with my patient and family as we walk the cancer journey together.

I spend my days facilitating transformation — letting go of the old way of seeing and being such that something new not only can emerge, but can develop strong roots. I know that in all that I do, Bernie walks beside me — part of the long lineage of healers from which I draw the strength to enter each patient's room with mercy and awareness as my most important tools.

The Miracle Tape

BY JANE UPCHURCH

I cannot wholeheartedly say I am grateful for having had cancer, but I am so deeply grateful for all it has taught me. I was diagnosed with breast cancer in January 2007. My first reaction was one of shock and disbelief. How could someone as robustly healthy as me have cancer? Before I knew it, the whole machine of cancer treatment had begun, and I was on chemotherapy before the tumor had even been found.

The first lucky moment was when a friend who had had breast cancer years before sent me a battered and yellowing copy of *Love, Medicine & Miracles*. At first I was not sure how it could help, but then I got to chapter 4. Bernie lists four important questions there to determine your attitude about yourself and your disease. The second question was, what happened to you in the year or two before your illness? I had to check what had happened to me in that time period, and a light went on in my head! It was like I had been struck by a thunderbolt. I checked my diaries and found twenty-six significant events, starting with the death of my father. I had been brought up to be strong, be independent, help others, and deal with events head on. Now I realized that all the deeply distressful events I thought I had dealt with had had a profound effect on my health. I fit the psychological profile of a cancer patient. I was gripped and read and reread the book during my chemotherapy. I also read every book by Bernie that I could lay my hands on and bought his CD to improve my immune system by meditation.

After my last chemo session I became very ill. The antibiotics were not controlling my temperature, and I knew I was getting worse when a microbiologist was called. I could not eat or sleep. I told my husband that if I got any worse, I was not sure I would have the stamina to get through it.

That night, as I could not sleep, I played Bernie's CD over and over again until I almost knew it word for word. It was Bernie's calm voice on the CD that allowed me to overcome the "challenge" that the disease offered me and be reassured that "your body knows what to do."

I must have fallen asleep eventually because when I woke up I knew something was different. I was going to recover. I told my husband I had "turned the corner." And although I had completely lost the independence I had spent my life acquiring, I did not care. Now I appreciated *everything*.

Some of Bernie's teachings carry me forward to this day. For instance, it is especially important to avoid negative messages, and there is nothing wrong with hope. Also, there are no incurable diseases, only incurable people. If one patient can do it, there's no reason others can't.

I do not think I would be alive if Bernie Siegel had not written *Love, Medicine & Miracles*. Even though we have never met, I feel he is a dear friend who inspires me completely. I will always be grateful to him for his wisdom and for showing me the way! I use Bernie's saying that "coincidence is God's way of remaining anonymous" every time a meaningful coincidence occurs in my life. For me, cancer wasn't a disease; it was the cure.

Miracle Memo

I have a sense of an energy field around some patients or people. When I felt this positive energy, I knew my patients were healing, and I would tell them the good news. It told me more than all the lab tests because I had experienced the truth of this feeling. My dog Buddy does the same thing when he walks around the room during a support group meeting. I can sense what he knows about the people in the room.

In Susan Duffy's case, *she* is the miracle. Despite coming from a difficult family, she chose life. Yes, I helped her because I was willing to listen to her and love the wounded child within her. When I asked her to bring me one of her baby pictures, she told me she didn't have any. So, I simply sat there when she displayed rage and anger at her painful life, and in the end this was what allowed her to empty out all the pain and begin to heal. She has become my teacher.

Her doctor told her, "All you've got is a hope and a prayer." When she asked him how to do that, he told her, "It's not my line." Well, she learned how and drove him nuts and is alive thirty years later. Why? As she wrote to me in a letter: "I grew up in a prison. I had no control over the parents who raised me, or the circumstances I was exposed to, but when I let love into my prison, it changed every negative item in it, meaning the experiences in my life, and turned them into something meaningful. And when I die, love will gently take me out of my prison and take me home with him where there are no prisons." She also advises that when you can love the unlovable and forgive the unforgivable, you are free.

When Jennifer Giuffre-Donohue sees positivity and inspiration in others, it is because they dwell within her. So what I use as a test of my own evolution is how nice other people seem to me. As the years go by and I work on myself, I find that the people I meet get nicer and nicer because my view of them has changed, and I am more loving and forgiving.

Of course, what Jennifer considers weird is normal. There are signs placed for all of us to see so that we stay on our path and find our way through life. Keep your eyes and ears open to the greater consciousness and let your awake mind and dreaming mind guide you and help you to heal. We are told God speaks in dreams and symbols, but listen for voices, too, telling you what path to follow. I hear them often and they have made my life more meaningful, peaceful, and joyful.

Our love is what makes us immortal. Jennifer can achieve that, as we all can, through her relationships with other living things of all species and through her writing. I see what my writing has done, when I hear from people all over the world thanking me for my words and how they have been helped by them.

Matt Mumber and I go way back together. I spoke at his medical school and got him to do the drawings he mentions. Part of the problem is that most professions present us with information, but they do not educate us as to why we chose that profession so that we would be emotionally healthier.

While in medical school, Matt started a group called GEMS, or Groups of Exceptional Medical Students. No one came to the meeting because their interpretation was that exceptional students got the highest grades. Matt had to define it as being for students who cared about people and not just the diagnosis, and then attendance went up.

We need to see that we are treating people; we are not just prescribing for what is wrong but asking how we can help our patients. When we love our patients, re-parent them and help them find new lives, miracles happen due to self-induced healing.

Matt's early drawings were of the specialties he was considering, and the healthiest picture showed him as a radiation oncologist and not a family doctor or surgeon. Without a drawing I would have thought family practice would be good for a man like him, but his intuition knows more than my intellect. In each picture he showed his future family with a wife and three children, and when he and his wife were concerned about having children, I guaranteed they would have three, and they do today.

The thing that makes us truly vulnerable — and this is not about blaming people — is what is going on in our lives and minds. When Jane Upchurch says she cherishes and appreciates everything, think about the message she is sending to every cell and gene in her body. Yes, I love life, and believe me, when you love your life, miracles happen!

You each hold the power, the beauty,
the fulfillment that only God can
bring — the courage, the hope,
the Glory of God instilled inside your heart
to ensure that miracles become your
everyday reality here on earth.
This is what I wish for you:
the security and bliss that only
your relationship
with God can bring.

Postscript

*A*s *we have seen in the stories,* miracles are a daily occurrence in all areas of our lives. Creation is a miracle. Life is a miracle. But I do think, from my experience on a personal level, that miracles require a certain set of conditions to occur. To simplify the requirements, I would say they basically consist of finding a sense of harmony and inner peace in your life. Two areas in which I have seen miracles occur, in both my life and my medical practice, are through dreams and drawings. The universal language of creation is symbols and images. I was a nonbeliever until I did some drawings for Elisabeth Kübler-Ross and was amazed at what they revealed about my life.

Dreams and drawings can reveal psychic and somatic information about our past, present, and future because unconsciously we are preparing the future. I want to leave you with some ideas and exercises so you can use drawings as a tool to help you create miracles in your life.

The real questions we must ask ourselves are, How does the invisible become visible? What is the language of creation and of the soul? How do psychics communicate with animals, distant individuals, and the dead? What sees when we have a near-death experience and leave our bodies? How does the community of cells speak to the conscious mind about its needs and health? How do we know what future plans our unconscious is creating?

By taking the lid off the unconscious, we can be guided by its wisdom and knowledge. It allows us to go within ourselves through the use of imagery and drawings. I have seen amazing outcomes through the use of these pathways of communicating with all parts of ourselves and the universe.

Rather than turn away from this kind of experience, or not accept it because we cannot explain or understand it, I, like the astronomers and quantum physicists, seek to explore the invisible and communicate with it through the language of creation.

As a surgeon I was not made aware in my training of the many uses of spontaneous and planned drawings. I have always been an artist and a visual person. In 1977 I attended a workshop presented by Dr. Carl Simonton, and in 1979 one presented by Dr. Elisabeth

Kübler-Ross. The former led to my first experience with guided imagery, and the latter with spontaneous drawing. Both revealed incredible insights and information about my life, and so I became a believer and returned to my practice, where a box of crayons became one of my therapeutic tools. I began to ask my patients and their families to draw pictures and to tell me about their dreams to help us make therapeutic decisions based upon not just intellect but inner knowingness, as well as to help family relationships and psychological issues. I was amazed by what I learned.

Gregg Furth, the author of *The Secret World of Drawings*, and Susan Bach, the author of *Life Paints Its Own Span*, both Jungian therapists, also helped guide me. I learned that there were many adults who were afraid to draw because they felt they were not artists and might get a poor grade in art. Children do not have that fear; they are not inhibited or self-conscious, and so it takes exceptional adults to be willing to share their drawings and want to learn from their inner wisdom or intuition, as well as their intellect.

Inner knowingness speaks a powerful language and can be used for prevention, treatment, diagnosis, and prognosis of an illness or emotional problem, as well as to make decisions, such as where to go to college, who to marry, whether to take chemotherapy, and what nutrition one needs. Very often what one fears may be portrayed in a drawing as very therapeutic, and the conflict between intellect and intuition resolves to the benefit of the patient.

Through drawings we can learn and discover what is within us and available to us. Drawing opened my mind and led me to pursue knowledge in a way that I had never been exposed to. I now refer to myself as a Jungian surgeon, and I use drawings in my therapy groups and through my website to help guide people in their lives and decision-making processes.

Symbols also open the door to something greater than any one person's wisdom. They connect us to our inner knowingness, creative instinct, rightness, and connection with our creative designer. This communication can be done anywhere on this planet, with anyone, because the symbols are a universal language, just as universal as our myths are. They can be miracle producing and require minimal supplies — crayons and paper.

Following is an exercise for you to experiment with and see what miracles appear in your life.

Miracle Drawing Exercise

First, make sure your crayons or colored pencils include all the colors of the rainbow plus black, white, and brown because every color has meaning. Then get some white paper to draw on. I am not going to tell you what the colors mean, or what different areas of the drawing represent time-wise, because I don't want you thinking about what you're creating. This should be a spontaneous drawing. Also, after you finish, I suggest you put the drawing away for a day or two before trying to interpret it. At that point, your unconscious will no longer be blinding you to what you drew, so you can learn from the symbols. Here are some options for you to consider, depending on which apply to your life and situation. This is not about your skill as an artist but about what your unconscious wants you to be made aware of. So don't ask your children to draw it for you.

1. Holding the page vertically, draw a picture of yourself. For all other drawings, hold the page horizontally. You can also do a separate drawing of yourself at work.

2. Draw your home and family, and be brave enough to ask your children to do it also.

3. Draw an outdoor scene you create from your imagination.

4. Draw a picture of any choices you are considering, from where to live, what job to take, and who to marry to anything else that is on your mind.

5. If you have a disease, you can draw yourself, your disease, your treatment, and your white blood cells eliminating the disease.

6. Draw something you are hoping and wishing for yourself and for someone else.

When you are done, and have waited a day, go over your drawings and ask your family to join you, if you are comfortable receiving their comments. Think of the many aspects of the drawings as representing you, just as a dream does. For help interpreting your drawings, read the books I mentioned on page 281 or get in touch with me through my website, www.berniesiegelmd.com.

Happy Miracles!

Bernie

Acknowledgments

I wish to offer special thanks to all the people who have opened their hearts and shared the stories of their lives with us. To Andrea Hurst for all the wisdom, time, and energy she gently provides, and to her assistant, Cate Perry, for her expert editing and for helping us hold things together while moving forward. To Cindy Hurn for her support, and to Georgia Hughes and all the wonderful people at New World Library, who are always a pleasure to work with, thank you. Most of all I am grateful and thankful for the conscious, intelligent, loving energy that created life and gave us the opportunity to share this miraculous and meaningful experience.

Contributors

The book's contributors are listed alphabetically by last name, with the page numbers of their stories on the right. In some cases, their websites, their email addresses, and titles of the books they've written are also included.

About Dr. Bernie S. Siegel

*D*r. *Bernie S. Siegel* is a well-known proponent of alternative approaches to healing that heal not just the body but the mind and soul. Bernie, as his friends and patients call him, attended Colgate University and studied medicine at Cornell University Medical College. His surgical training took place at Yale New Haven Hospital, West Haven Veteran's Hospital, and the Children's Hospital of Pittsburgh. In 1978 Bernie pioneered a new approach to group and individual cancer therapy called ECaP (Exceptional Cancer Patients) that utilized patients' drawings, dreams, and feelings, and he broke new ground in facilitating important patient lifestyle changes and engaging the patient in the healing process. Bernie retired from general and pediatric surgical practice in 1989. Always a strong advocate for his patients, Bernie has since dedicated himself to humanizing the medical establishment's approach to patients and empowering patients to play a vital role in the process of self-induced healing to achieve their greatest potential. He continues to run support groups and is an active speaker, traveling around the world to address patient and caregiver groups. As the author of several books, including *Love, Medicine & Miracles*; *Peace, Love & Healing*; *How to Live Between Office Visits*; and *365 Prescriptions for the Soul*, Bernie has been at the forefront of the medical ethics and spiritual issues of our day. He and his wife (and occasional coauthor), Bobbie, live in a suburb of New Haven, Connecticut. They have five children, eight grandchildren, four cats, two dogs, and much love. Visit his website at www.berniesiegelmd.com.

About Andrea Hurst

*A*ndrea Hurst *has worked in the publishing business* for over thirty years as an author, literary agent, and consultant. Working with Bernie on this heartfelt collection was serendipitous for her after experiencing her own healing miracles with the help of Bernie's first book, *Love, Medicine & Miracles.* Her first published book, *Everybody's Natural Foods Cookbook,* was followed by the insightful and humorous *The Lazy Dog's Guide to Enlightenment.* Her articles on book publishing have appeared in *Writer's Digest* magazine and *The Complete Handbook of Novel Writing.* Andrea is a keynote speaker and educator at writers' conferences and is the founder of www.justwriteon.com, a website that offers expert instruction and resources for writers. She is an adjunct faculty member for the Northwest Institute of Literary Arts MFA Program in creative writing, and she enjoys working with authors who are driven by their enthusiasm to create books that touch lives and make a difference.

NEW WORLD LIBRARY is dedicated to publishing books and other media that inspire and challenge us to improve the quality of our lives and the world.

We are a socially and environmentally aware company, and we strive to embody the ideals presented in our publications. We recognize that we have an ethical responsibility to our customers, our staff members, and our planet.

We serve our customers by creating the finest publications possible on personal growth, creativity, spirituality, wellness, and other areas of emerging importance. We serve New World Library employees with generous benefits, significant profit sharing, and constant encouragement to pursue their most expansive dreams.

As a member of the Green Press Initiative, we print an increasing number of books with soy-based ink on 100 percent postconsumer-waste recycled paper. Also, we power our offices with solar energy and contribute to nonprofit organizations working to make the world a better place for us all.

Our products are available
in bookstores everywhere.
For our catalog, please contact:

New World Library
14 Pamaron Way
Novato, California 94949

Phone: 415-884-2100 or 800-972-6657
Catalog requests: Ext. 50
Orders: Ext. 52
Fax: 415-884-2199
Email: escort@newworldlibrary.com

To subscribe to our electronic newsletter, visit
www.newworldlibrary.com

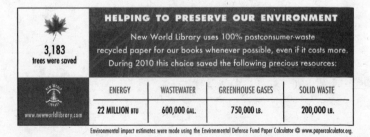